WITHDRAWN

Wren

Hanc Tabulam invenit & incepit Anton: Verrio, Perfecerunt Gothofredus Kneller & Joc: Thornhill Equites.

1 Sir Christopher Wren by Antonio Verrio, Sir Godfrey Kneller and Sir James Thornhill

Wren

MARGARET WHINNEY

166 illustrations

THAMES AND HUDSON
LONDON

To Ellis Waterhouse
in gratitude for much help
over many years

© 1971 THAMES AND HUDSON LTD, LONDON

Printed in Great Britain by Jarrold and Sons Ltd, Norwich

ISBN 0 500 18118 7 *clothbound*
ISBN 0 500 20112 9 *paperbound*

Contents

Author's acknowledgments   6

CHAPTER I
Early years   7

CHAPTER II
The turn to architecture   25

CHAPTER III
The City churches   45

CHAPTER IV
The planning of St Paul's   81

CHAPTER V
The building of St Paul's   97

CHAPTER VI
Secular buildings before 1688   133

CHAPTER VII
The mature secular buildings   161

CHAPTER VIII
Conclusion   193

Chronological table   204

Bibliography   206

Illustration acknowledgments   208

List of illustrations   209

Index   213

Author's acknowledgments

My thanks are due to many people who, throughout my life, have taught me about Wren, and especially to my father, the late Professor Geoffrey Webb and Sir John Summerson. Sir Anthony Blunt and Professor Rudolf Wittkower have constantly enlarged my knowledge of Continental architecture. More specific thanks are due to Professor and Mrs Peter Murray and Dr Kerry Downes for constant help in discussion; while my debt to Miss Elizabeth Clarke for her endless help and patience over the collection of plates is one which I hope the appearance of the book will partly, but not wholly repay.

M. D. W.

CHAPTER ONE

Early years

Sir Christopher Wren made himself into a great architect. He had no formal training and little opportunity of knowing, at first-hand, the architecture of the Continent of his own or any other age. He built nothing before he was thirty; but by the time he was seventy and still very active, he could rival any European architect then living. He was presented with remarkable opportunities, for he was called upon to design a great number of buildings widely differing in size and intention; and by a process of trial and error, and above all of retrial, he learnt from his opportunities until he became a master of his art. One of his outstanding characteristics throughout his life was indeed his willingness to produce a scheme, to abandon it if it proved impractical, and to go on working on a problem, often even during execution, until something both satisfactory and possible had been achieved. His work cannot, in fact, be fully appreciated without some reference to discarded schemes, for it is here that the striking flexibility of his mind is best displayed. It enabled him to achieve a great range of buildings, some less magnificent than he might have wished, but supremely well suited to their purpose and to the circumstances which controlled their execution.

Christopher Wren was born in 1632, in the most tranquil years of the reign of Charles I. His family had close contact with the court, for though at the time of his birth his father was Rector of East Knoyle, Wiltshire, he was very soon to succeed his brother Matthew as Dean of Windsor and Registrar of the Order of the Garter. Both brothers, Royalist and High Church, were to suffer for their opinions during the Civil War. The Dean's house was twice sacked, and he had to flee, first to the West Country and then to his son-in-law, William Holder, at

Bletchingdon in Oxfordshire, where he died in 1656. Matthew, by then Bishop of Ely, had a harder fate, for he was imprisoned for eighteen years in the Tower of London. It may well be that the recollection of the troubled years of his boyhood was to strengthen Christopher's tendency to moderation. Later in life he was to serve the Crown for nearly fifty years, but in spite of the changes in the monarchy and the turbulent political and religious situation in England after the death of Charles II, Wren stood apart from these storms and, staying in office, went steadily on with his work.

Partly because of the Civil War, which broke out when he was ten years old, the precise course of his early education is obscure. He spent some time at Westminster School, under the famous headmaster, Dr Busby, but he appears also to have learnt much from his brother-in-law, William Holder. At some time in the late 1640s he went to Wadham College, Oxford, taking his degree there in 1651. He was still working at Oxford in 1654 as a Fellow of All Souls, when John Evelyn, the diarist who was to become a personal friend, makes his first reference to him as 'that miracle of a youth, Mr Christopher Wren'.

The field in which the young man was using his remarkable talents was not in the arts, but in science. It must be remembered that in the seventeenth century there was not the deep cleavage between the two fields which exists today, and that Wren, like all other scholars of his time, had a good classical education. Indeed, he was to show himself a fine Latinist. On the other hand, the foundations of modern science were laid in the seventeenth century, which was particularly notable for the invention of new apparatus with which scientific problems could be investigated. Logarithms, algebra, the slide-rule and the microscope were all in use for the first time, and through careful study of lenses, great improvements were made to the telescope. The last was of special importance to Wren, who devoted much time to the study of astronomy. In 1657, when he was only twenty-five, he was appointed Professor of Astronomy at Gresham College, London. This college, founded under the will of the great Elizabethan merchant, Sir Thomas Gresham, was not part of a university, but provided lectures on seven subjects, the professors being appointed by the Corporation of London and the Mercers' Company. Unfortunately, only his Inaugural Lecture at Gresham College has survived, but it is revealing. The City Fathers had given him his appointment, and he dwells on the advantages to navigation, and therefore to trade, of the study of astronomy. And he also defines the great significance which, since the work of Descartes, had been given to scientific truth: 'Mathematical Demonstrations being built upon the impregnable foundations of Geometry and Arithmetick, are the only Truths, that can sink into the mind of man, void of all uncertainty; and all other Discourses participate more or less of Truth, according as Their Subjects are more or less capable of Mathematical Demonstration.' The Age of Reason has its foundations in seventeenth-century thought, which held that all could be explained by scientific method, and used for the greater happiness of mankind.

Wren's scientific work ranged over a variety of fields beyond that of astronomy, and included optics, meteorology, physiology and the laws of motion, but astronomy has a special significance for his later career, since his work frequently entailed the making of models. At Oxford, he had formed one of a group of scientists who met regularly to discuss their work. After 1657 the meetings took place in Gresham College, London, and very soon after the Restoration of Charles II in 1660, they formed themselves into a society which gained the King's interest and was granted a Charter in March 1661 as the Royal Society. It is still the most distinguished scientific society in the world. In the same year Wren left London, for he was appointed Savilian Professor of Astronomy at Oxford, in succession to his teacher, Dr Seth Ward.

This background of science, though it cannot be discussed in any detail here, is crucial for an understanding of Wren's career. He was an active member of the Royal Society for many years after he had left science for architecture, and was to

9

be its President in 1681. His most intimate friends were scientists, and he therefore moved in a world in which problems of many kinds and their possible method of solution were ceaselessly discussed. His own contribution was clearly considerable, for Sir Isaac Newton in his *Principia* of 1687 was to speak of him as one of the three greatest geometers of the age. It can hardly be doubted that it was Wren's training in science which enabled him to formulate a problem, and to experiment with great flexibility of mind until it was solved. And his genius for mathematics enabled him to face and overcome constructional problems on a scale so far unknown in England.

His connection with the Royal Society also brought him into personal touch with the King. Charles had an inquisitive mind, and Wren, who had early shown his ability as a draughtsman in the illustrations to the *Cerebri Anatome* by an Oxford scientist, Dr Willis, presented the King with a series of drawings of insects seen through the microscope. Soon afterwards he made for him a large-scale model of the moon. He must have impressed Charles as a man of great and practical talents, with a wide range of interests, for in 1661 he was invited to take charge of the fortifications of Tangier, that city being part of the dowry of Charles's Queen, Catherine of Braganza. He excused himself on grounds of health and continued his work at Oxford, but very soon his abilities led to other calls on his time. By 1663 he had designed his first important building.

Much of our information concerning Wren's work comes from drawings, building accounts and contemporary documents, such as letters or other men's diaries. But one important source of a different kind exists, and will often be quoted. In 1750 Wren's grandson, Stephen, was to publish *Parentalia*, containing lives of his grandfather and Bishop Matthew Wren. Much of the information about Sir Christopher was put together by his son (also called Christopher) partly in 1728, five years after the old man's death, and partly in 1741. The younger Christopher had worked with his father towards the end of his life, and his evidence on the later works is therefore first-hand. The account of the earlier works was probably derived from his father's memories or from friends, but even so it is the major source for the architect's career.

English architecture at the time Wren began to build was in a somewhat confused state, and there was no clearly recognizable national style. Moreover, owing to the social and political history of the previous hundred years, it was provincial and indeed grossly old-fashioned by Continental standards. In the sixteenth century the forms and ideals of Italian Renaissance architecture had spread to northern Europe. But in the England of Elizabeth I, Italian architectural theory rooted in antiquity was scarcely known, for travel to Italy was not encouraged for political reasons, and though the forms (for instance, the orders of architecture) were recognized, they were used as decoration rather than as an integral part of the structure. Such decoration was frequently clumsy and coarse, and was copied from German or Flemish books of engravings.

Before the death of Elizabeth I in 1603, the great artist who was to change the standard of English architecture had already paid his first visit to Italy. Inigo Jones (1573–1652) had not yet begun to work as an architect but was very soon to introduce up-to-date Continental devices into his designs for court masques. In 1615, after a further visit to Italy, he was given the office of Surveyor to the Crown, which placed him in charge of all royal building. During this last visit to Italy, Jones had paid deep attention to the architecture of antiquity, and also to that of the sixteenth-century architect, Andrea Palladio, whose reverence for antiquity was clearly displayed in his buildings and in his publication, *I Quattro Libri dell'Architettura* (1570). Jones was to use the book throughout his career, and almost all his architecture is based on Palladian sources.

His buildings must have seemed revolutionary to the English. Perhaps the most striking, and certainly the most influential, was the new Banqueting House for Whitehall Palace of 1619–21. In its emphasis on a system of related proportions, which govern every part of the building, its skilful use of   *Ill. 3*

2 Inigo Jones. Banqueting House, Whitehall

3 Inigo Jones.
Banqueting House, Whitehall

superimposed orders set against the channelled wall, in the regularity and sobriety of the window design and the restrained use of decorative detail, it shows that Jones had completely absorbed Italian theory, and Italian forms, and could use his knowledge to create a new and original work. The inside, re- *Ill. 2* cently beautifully restored, is an enormous single room, the proportions being a double cube, which in the 1630s was to be covered with Rubens' great ceiling showing the glorification of the House of Stuart. As will be seen later, it is certain that Wren greatly admired the Banqueting House, and, since he was never to visit Italy, it was partly from this design of Inigo Jones that he must have derived his knowledge of the standards of Italian architecture.

Although Jones was to remain Surveyor to the Crown throughout the reign of Charles I, sadly little of his work remains. The Queen's House at Greenwich (now part of the National Maritime Museum) is an Italian villa on English soil, and the Queen's Chapel at St James's, with its great coffered vault taken from Palladio, has a dignity beyond its size.

Ill. 4 Occasionally, he worked for private clients. St Paul's, Covent Garden, an exercise in the Tuscan order, was built for the Earl of Bedford. It was the first parish church in the classical style to be built in England, and the first to be part of a formal layout. The Piazza, as it was called, has now disappeared and the church is largely rebuilt, but the new regularized town-planning and the simple, flat-fronted houses, were to influence much later building. The last important building by Jones was the great Corinthian portico which he added in the 1630s to Old St Paul's, but his work on the Cathedral will be better discussed in the next chapter.

Jones trained one pupil, John Webb (1611–72), who worked with him from 1628, and was regarded as his deputy. A great number of drawings, some by Jones, but many more by Webb, have survived for unexecuted buildings. Some, such as the designs for churches and ideal palaces, may be for illustrations to a book which was never written; others are for vast rebuilding schemes for Whitehall Palace. These drawings are well known in the late seventeenth and eighteenth centuries, and it will be shown later that Wren must at some time have had access to them.

The new style of Jones and Webb hardly spread beyond the court. The influence it may have had on country-house architecture does not concern us here, since Wren was not a country-house architect. And after the outbreak of the Civil War in 1642, no major public building was undertaken until the 1660s. In Jones's lifetime, however, work was produced by less sophisticated designers, often though not always in brick, and continuing, but in a more restrained fashion, the Flemish type of decorative detail used by the Elizabethans. Moreover, one

PIAZZA in Conventgarden.

4 Inigo Jones. St Paul's, Covent Garden

Italian pattern book was now available for designers who found the Flemish taste too flamboyant, for in 1611 part of the works of Sebastiano Serlio had been translated from the Dutch edition by Robert Peake. This provided, for those who cared to use it, information about the buildings of antiquity as well as a number of designs for gates, fireplaces, and other details in the manner of mid-sixteenth-century Italy. The more complete Italian edition was also available. Though it was probably the most popular, Serlio's was not the only illustrated book available to architects and patrons. Other sixteenth-century architects, such as Vignola and Philibert de l'Orme, had published treatises in their own languages, though neither seems to have been widely used in England. A far more important work, which had immense prestige as the only surviving architectural book of antiquity, was Vitruvius' *De Architectura Libri X*, of which a fine Italian edition had been published by Daniele Barbaro in Venice in 1556, followed by a Latin edition in 1567.

This was certainly used in England, and may well have been Wren's first means of introduction to classical architecture. He would probably also have read Sir Henry Wotton's *Elements of Architecture* of 1624, a work which draws freely on Italian Renaissance theory.

At the Restoration of Charles II in 1660, the royal Office of Works had to be reconstituted. John Webb, not unreasonably, hoped for the Surveyorship, for he was undoubtedly the best-trained architect in England. But Charles decided to grant the offices to men who had served him in exile. The Surveyorship was given to Sir John Denham, a not undistinguished poet, but an untried architect, though by 1664 Webb was referred to as Deputy-Surveyor-General. The Paymastership went to Hugh May, who had been trained as a painter in the studio of Sir Peter Lely, but who was to show himself an architect of some ability.

One other architect of some experience, Sir Roger Pratt, was working in this decade. He had travelled in Italy and France, and was in touch with Jones, though to what extent is not clear, over the building of Coleshill House in Berkshire (now destroyed), a work of considerable distinction. All his known work was domestic, and he was to retire from professional life in 1667 when he inherited the family estates. He left notebooks which show that he did not entirely lose contact with architecture, and his criticisms of Wren's early work at St Paul's are of interest in view of his knowledge of Continental architecture.

The only major royal building which was put in hand in the early 1660s was a new palace at Greenwich. Charles had, during his exile, acquired a liking for yachting and wished for a palace where he could enjoy it. The Queen's House was too small for the court, and the old Tudor palace nearer the river, much favoured by Queen Elizabeth I, was in poor repair. A new palace was designed by John Webb, the foundations being laid in 1664. Two blocks, flanking a court running down to the river, were planned, with a third block surmounted by a low dome linking them at the inner end of the court, thus blocking the view from the Queen's House to the river. Only the western block, known

5 John Webb. King Charles's Block, Greenwich

Ill. 5

as King Charles's Block, was completed by the King. It is a building of real distinction, with its strong effect of mass and its finely balanced horizontals and verticals. And it is very different in scale and conception from Inigo Jones's Banqueting House. The earlier work is a clearly defined two-storey design, made up of small units, which could if necessary be increased or curtailed without fundamentally altering the design. King Charles's Block is a large-scale single unit, tied together at centre and ends by a giant order, and no part could be added or taken away without destroying the conception of the whole. Jones's, in fact, is still a Renaissance building, whereas Webb has moved a long way towards the Baroque. It is beyond question the most accomplished building, in its mastery of architectural forms, to be erected in England in the 1660s, and sets a standard against which Wren's early work must be judged.

6 Hugh May.
Eltham Lodge, Kent

7 Jacob van Campen and
Pieter Post. Mauritshuis,
The Hague

Hugh May created no major building in this decade, but
Ill. 6 Eltham Lodge, Kent, the house he built for a City magnate, Sir
John Shaw, demands a brief mention for the new influence it
reveals. May, like many other members of the court, had
visited Holland during the exile, and this house of brick, with
giant stone pilasters supporting the pediment which breaks up
Ill. 7 into the hipped roof, has much in common with the Mauritshuis
at The Hague, which all English exiles must have known. From
now on Dutch influence superseded Flemish, and, as will be
shown, Wren was not untouched by it.

It is not clear precisely why Wren first turned to architecture, but it may well have been that, since he was known as a gifted mathematician with a strongly practical turn of mind, he was consulted over problems of construction. There is reason to believe that as early as 1661, about the time of the Tangier project, he was asked to advise on the condition of Old St Paul's. (His proposals will be discussed in Chapter II.) But it was at Oxford that he had his first opportunity of mastering an architectural problem.

Gilbert Sheldon, formerly Warden of All Souls College, but by now Bishop of London, had determined that University ceremonies, which till then had taken place in St Mary's Church, would be more fittingly housed in a new secular building. In April 1663, at a meeting of the Royal Society, Wren showed a model of the building which was to be known as the Sheldonian Theatre. The foundation-stone was laid in *Ill. 8* June 1664, and John Evelyn records that the first ceremony was held in it in 1669. The basic requirement was for a building of considerable size, capable of holding a great number of people who could watch the proceedings. Wren turned to antiquity for his pattern, and planned his building on the lines of the Theatre of Marcellus in Rome, which he would have known *Ill. 9* from the engraving in Serlio. It was a form admirably fitted to the purpose, since the ceremonies could take place on the stage at the flattened end, and the spectators sit in the semicircle. Roman theatres were, however, open to the sky, or covered by a *velarium* or awning to keep off the sun; but any building in England had to be roofed. Here was Wren's first major architectural problem. The building was 70 feet wide, the space being *Ill. 10* therefore too great for a single beam of wood. Either supports must rise from the floor, and spoil the spectators' view, or some other solution must be found. Wren found it by devising an ingenious truss on a triangulation system. The timbers of the *Ill. 11* ceiling were dovetailed together, and held in place by an upright in the centre (hidden from below by the ceiling), which was itself supported by sloping beams on either side, under the

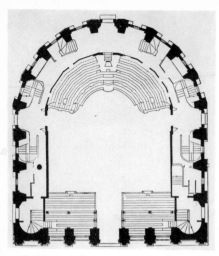

8 Sheldonian Theatre, Oxford. Plan

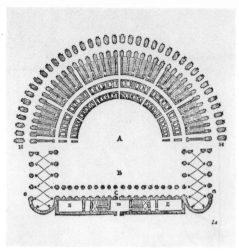

9 Plan of the Theatre of Marcellus in Rome

10 Sheldonian Theatre, Oxford

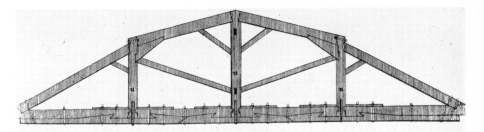

11 Sheldonian Theatre, Oxford. Roof truss

12 Sheldonian Theatre, Oxford, from the north. The oval windows above the balustrade were removed in 1802, and the cupola redesigned in 1838

13 Sheldonian Theatre, Oxford, from the south.

roof. The system is not far from that used in some of the open-trussed roofs of late medieval churches in East Anglia, but it is said to have been taken by Wren from an invention of his former Professor of Geometry, Dr John Wallis, known as the 'Geometrical Flat Floor', but reversed, and put at the top of the building instead of below. The idea of the Roman theatre is, however, evident in the decoration of the ceiling, which was painted by Robert Streeter with the representation of a great awning rolled back on cords (which in fact mark the joining of the beams) while above, on clouds against the painted sky, are allegorical figures showing the Triumph of Truth and the Arts.

The ceiling must have had considerable strength, for the building originally housed the Clarendon Press; and the attics, then lit by oval windows above the balustrade which have now disappeared, were used as a book store, while the printing-presses were in the basement.

This interior is a *tour de force* which amazed and delighted Wren's contemporaries. The exterior, on the other hand, reveals his inexperience as an architect. The account of the building in *Parentalia* implies that he had wished the outside, as well as the inside, to follow the pattern of the Theatre of Marcellus, but that it proved too expensive. The Roman theatre has a fine design, not unlike that of the Colosseum though on a smaller scale, of superimposed orders with arches between, which is dignified in itself, and very suitable for a rounded

Ill. 12 building. Wren's compromise is curiously flat and lacking in monumentality. The division into two unequal storeys is reasonable enough, taking into account the disposition of the gallery inside, and the arrangement for lighting the interior; but the arches in the lower storey are hardly more than surface decoration, and the upper windows are not very happy in proportion. And the reduction of the curve to a series of flat surfaces was no doubt practical on grounds of cost, but it seems more than a little gauche.

Ill. 13 For the flat end of the building, Wren had allowed himself a double order of superimposed half-columns and pilasters under a large and smaller pediment. The main design is based fairly closely on a plate in Serlio for a Venetian portico, but Wren is not yet very competent in his handling of detail, and the organization of the upper row of windows, which ends in panels, is somewhat crude. A comparison of the exterior of this building with John Webb's King Charles's Block at Greenwich *Ill. 5* shows that, at the beginning of his career, Wren was very far from Webb's mastery of architectural forms and treatment of masses. Nevertheless, the size and ingenuity of the interior far outweighed the immaturity of the exterior, and provided his friends with some indication of the ability of the yet untried architect.

Two smaller University commissions were in hand before 1665. The Chapel of Pembroke College, Cambridge, conse- *Ill. 14*

14 Pembroke College
Chapel, Cambridge

crated in 1664, was the gift of Bishop Matthew Wren. It was originally a simple rectangle (the present chancel was added in the nineteenth century) with a fine plaster ceiling. It presented no problems of construction, but it is distinguished by a well-designed front to the street, with four giant pilasters under a pediment. Again the idea is based on a design from Serlio, but its adaptation is more skilful than that at Oxford.

The remaining building, of which only part remains, was a block of lodgings at Trinity College, Oxford. The design was simple, plain walls with no orders, and a hipped roof. Again Wren was building for a friend, for the President of the College was Dr Ralph Bathurst, a member of that Oxford scientific circle which preceded the establishment of the Royal Society. The block was completed in 1668, and though letters exist to show that Wren was consulted about later works at the College, including the Chapel, there is no evidence that these were carried out from his design.

CHAPTER TWO

The turn to architecture

On 22 June 1665, while discussion was still taking place over the extent of the building at Trinity College, Oxford, Wren wrote to Dr Bathurst, saying that he would be in Paris within a fortnight. Only a few of his letters have survived, and this one is interesting on personal grounds for, like his portraits, it reveals his sense of humour, and also his willingness to poke fun at academic argument. And it proves beyond doubt that architecture had become a serious concern with him, for he speaks of his expectation of meeting 'Mons. Mansart' and 'Signor Bernini'. It is, therefore, almost certain that he had provided himself with introductions to them, for neither François Mansart nor Gianlorenzo Bernini, both outstanding architects and both arrogant men, were particularly likely to have given time to an English scientist unknown to them.

Wren's visit to France, which was to last until the spring of 1666, was crucial for his career as an architect. It was the only opportunity he had, in his long life, of travelling on the Continent and of seeing modern buildings by architects of talent. Unfortunately he did not keep a diary, but one long and very revealing letter to an unknown correspondent is printed in *Parentalia*, though the original is now lost, and there are one or two letters from other travellers which refer to his activities. One of these, from the Secretary of the Royal Society, relates that a Parisian friend had taken Wren to call on several mathematicians, of whose work he approved, though he wished also to see their experiments. And, as he expected, he had met Bernini. Another letter from a young traveller, Edward Browne, the son of the famous physician, Sir Thomas Browne, tells of a three days' journey with Wren to see houses northeast of Paris – Chantilly, Liancourt, Verneuil and Le Raincy. The

15 Pierre Lescot. Great Court of the Louvre, Paris

last, by Louis Le Vau, with a fine domed saloon, seems to have pleased Wren most.

Ill. 15 Wren's own letter is too long to quote in full, though it is of great interest. He writes of going daily to watch the work on the Louvre, where the extension of the Great Court was not yet completed. He was struck with the large number of men employed, with the machines, or 'Engines', for raising stones, and by the regular visits of Colbert, the Surintendant des Bâtiments. He saw Bernini's design for the east front (the main reason for the great artist's journey to Paris), and adds: 'I would have given my skin for it, but the old reserved Italian gave me but a few Minutes View: it was five little designs in Paper, for which he hath received as many thousand Pistoles; I had only time to copy it in my Fancy and Memory; I shall be able by Discourse, and a Crayon, to give you a tolerable Account of it.' He spoke rather slightingly of Le Vau's Collège de France, of which he thought: 'the Artist hath purposely set it ill-favouredly, that he might show his Wit in struggling with an inconvenient situation'; but his enthusiasm was great for 'the glorious Appartment of the Queen Mother in the Louvre' and for its contents.

26

He records visits to many places outside Paris. Versailles was *Ill. 16* in 1665 still the small hunting-lodge of Louis XIII, but it pleased him greatly. Indeed his description contains one of his few major comments on architectural style: 'The Palace, or if you please, the Cabinet of Versailles call'd me twice to view it: the mixtures of Brick, Stone, blue Tile and Gold make it look like a rich Livery: not an inch within but is crowded with little Curiosities of Ornaments: the Women, as they make here the Language and Fashions, and meddle with Politicks and Philosophy, so they sway also in Architecture; works of Filgrand and little Knacks are in Great Vogue; but Building certainly ought to have the Attribute of eternal, and therefore the only Thing uncapable of new Fashions.' Finally, he lists a number of other buildings he had seen, including 'the incomparable Villas of Vaux and Maisons', and adds: 'and that I might not lose the Impressions of them, I shall bring you almost all France in Paper, which I found by some or others ready design'd to my Hand, in which I have spent both Labour and some Money'. The collection of engravings to which this sentence must refer cannot now be traced, but, as will be seen, Wren was to make free use of them in some of his own designs.

16 Pierre Patel's painting of Versailles, *c.* 1668. The buildings are as Wren saw them, with the brick and stone hunting-lodge of Louis XIII in the centre, flanked by service wings added by Louis XIV between 1663 and 1665. The gardens were more modest, the elaborate layout of fountains and the Grand Canal dating from 1666 to 1668

17 Jacques Lemercier.
Church of the Sorbonne,
Paris

It would seem that Wren's unknown correspondent was only
interested in secular buildings, for no churches are mentioned
in the letter. There can, however, be no shadow of doubt that
they must have been a revelation to him. The only ecclesiastical
buildings in the classical style which he could have seen in
England were Inigo Jones's small chapel at St James's, and his
church of St Paul's, Covent Garden, an exceptionally austere
building. But in Paris he saw, for the only time in his life,
churches which were Baroque in conception and in decoration,
and which were domed. It is true that Wren might possibly
have seen a group of drawings of ideal churches by John Webb,
some of which were domed, but the difference between looking
at a drawing of a dome, and standing underneath the lofty
enclosed space of an executed dome, is enormous, and this new
experience must have been an exciting one for Wren. The two
Ill. 17 major domed churches of Paris were Lemercier's church of the
Ill. 18 Sorbonne, and the Val-de-Grâce, begun to the designs of
François Mansart, but completed according to those of
Ill. 19 Lemercier. The latter was not quite finished in 1665, but the

28

18 François Mansart and Jacques Lemercier. Church of the Val-de-Grâce, Paris

19 François Mansart and Jacques Lemercier. Church of the Val-de-Grâce, Paris

Questo è il diritto di dentro, & di fuori della pianta passata, dal qual si può comprendere la gran massa, & il gran peso che saria questo edificio sopra a quattro pilastri di tanta altezza: la qual massa (sì come io dissi auanti) doueria mettere pensiero ad ogni prudente Architetto a farla al piano di terra, non che in tanta altezza: & però io giudico, che l'Architetto dee esser piu presto alquanto timido che troppo animoso: perche se sarà timido, egli farà le sue cose ben sicure, & anco non sdegnerà di uolere il consiglio d'altri, e così facendo rare uolte perirà: ma se sarà troppo animoso, egli non uorrà l'altrui consiglio: anzi si considerà solamente nel suo ingegno, onde spesse volte precipitaranno le cose da lui fatte. & però io concludo che la troppo animosità proceda dalla presuntione, & la presuntione dal poco sapere: ma che la timidità sia cosa uirtuosa, dandosi sempre a credere di sapere o nulla, o poco. Le misure di questa opera si trouueranno con i palmi piccioli, che sono qui a dietro.

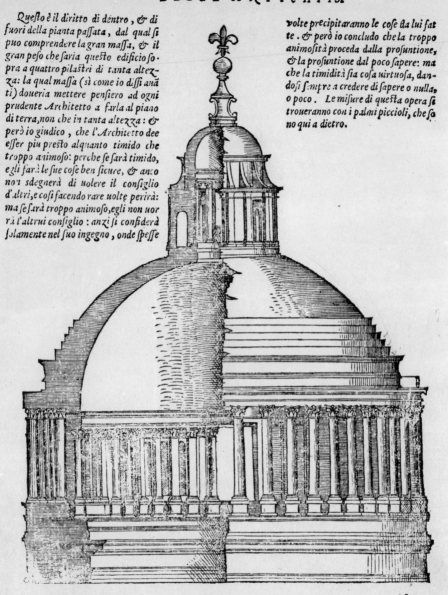

20 Bramante's design for the dome of St Peter's, Rome

21 Michelangelo's design for the dome of St Peter's, Rome

dome painting had been executed by Pierre Mignard in 1663, so the total effect could already be seen. There was also François Mansart's small domed church of the Visitation, with its ring of oval chapels, and Wren probably knew something of the as yet unfinished church of Sainte Anne-la-Royale, designed by the Italian Guarini, which had a surprising and complex arrangement of a ribbed dome with a smaller dome and lantern above it.

All seventeenth-century domes were basically derived from one of two models – either Bramante's unexecuted design for *Ill. 20* St Peter's, Rome, which was engraved in Serlio's treatise, or the executed dome designed by Michelangelo and carried out by *Ill. 21* Giacomo della Porta. The first was a hemisphere above a drum decorated with an evenly spaced ring of columns running round it. The executed dome was taller, with ribs on the exterior making a visual connection between drum, dome and the lantern above, and the drum, instead of presenting an endless circular rhythm, had paired columns with the entablature broken forward above them, thus stressing the vertical rather than the horizontal axis. In France, the executed dome of St

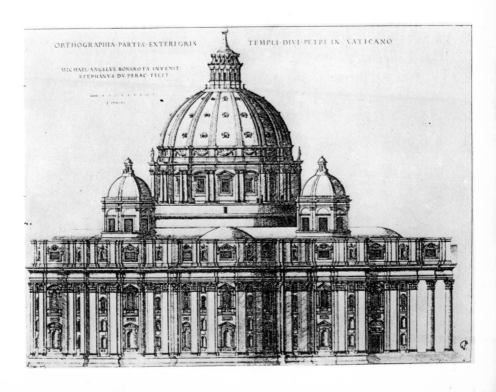

ORTHOGRAPHIA·PARTIS·EXTERIORIS   TEMPLI·DIVI·PETRI·IN·VATICANO

MICHAEL·ANGELVS·BONAROTA·INVENIT
STEPHANVS·DV·PERAC·FECIT

Peter's, rather than Bramante's more static conception, provided the chief inspiration for architects. And since the idea of a great domed building was to occupy much of Wren's mind during the next forty years, the impact of what he had seen in France was inevitably of great importance.

One very different type of ecclesiastical building must surely have been known to him, for like John Evelyn before him he must have visited the church of the French Protestants, the *Ill. 22* Temple at Charenton. This simple building was a rectangular hall, with galleries all round it, and the pulpit in the position normally occupied by the altar. Its arrangement may well have been stored in Wren's mind when he came to consider the needs of Protestant worship.

Wren's visit to Paris fell at a fortunate moment, for he escaped the Great Plague which ravaged England in 1665. He returned in the spring of 1666, and almost immediately presented a report on the condition of Old St Paul's, a subject which had *Ill. 23* concerned him for some time. The medieval Cathedral, with its Romanesque nave and Gothic choir had, earlier in the century,

22 Watercolour of Salomon de Brosse's Protestant Temple, Charenton

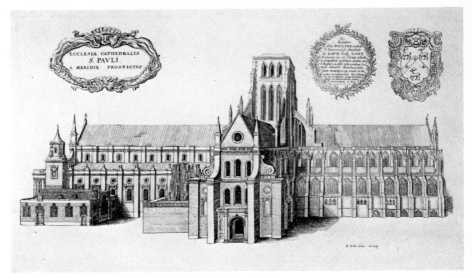

23 Hollar's engraving of Old St Paul's, London

been in need of repair. Inigo Jones, in the 1630s, had recased the nave, using classical pilasters in place of buttresses, and built a great Corinthian portico at the west end. Scaffolding had been then set up round the central tower, which was in poor condition, but the Civil War broke out in 1642, and nothing more was done. In 1663 a Royal Commission had been set up to consider the structure, which had deteriorated still further. Wren was not an original member, for he was scarcely yet known as an architect, but there is evidence that he was consulted before the end of the year.

The older men in the Commission, Sir John Denham the Surveyor, John Webb and Sir Roger Pratt, were in favour of patching up the old building, but Wren's report of May 1666 made much more drastic proposals. He suggested that the inside *Ill. 25* of the nave should be refaced like the outside, and that the nave vault should be replaced by saucer domes. He noted that it would be 'easy to perform it after a good Roman manner, so as to follow the Gothic rudeness of the old design'; and the beautiful drawings which accompanied the report show that by

33

24 Jacques Lemercier. Church of the
Sorbonne, Paris. Section

this he meant to rearrange the interior elevation by eliminating
the triforium and by throwing its space into the main arcade.
But his ideas for the central feature were much more revolutionary. He proposed to enlarge the crossing by cutting out the
inner piers and to cover the great central space resulting from
this by a high dome. 'The outward appearance of the church
will seem to swell in the middle by degrees to a large basis,
rising to a rotondo bearing a cupola, and then ending in the
lantern; and is with incomparable more grace in the remote
aspect than it is possible for the lean shaft of a steeple to afford.'
That sentence could scarcely have been written before the visit
to Paris, and it proves that, however much Wren may have
been concerned with structural problems, he was also deeply
aware, from the outset of his career, with visual effect. His
report also had practical suggestions, for the old tower was to be
used as scaffolding for the new dome, and then demolished, and
expense could also be saved by using methods of raising material
which he had learnt abroad.

34

25 St Paul's Cathedral. Pre-Fire design

These proposals contain two main ideas – a great central space and a tall dome – which were to dominate almost all Wren's plans for the Cathedral. It may well be that the combination of a central space with a Latin cross plan was first suggested to him by Ely Cathedral, the only English medieval building which includes these features. His uncle, Bishop Matthew Wren, had been Bishop of Ely, so Wren must have known the Cathedral, whose great octagonal lantern covers the crossing which is the full width of nave and aisles. But the authority for his dome is partly Italian and partly French. The high drum has an evenly spaced ring of columns round it, and therefore is derived from Bramante's dome for St Peter's, and above it are stepped-back rings of masonry which come from the same source. The tall dome above has, however, nothing to do with Bramante, but is basically Michelangelesque. The section, on the other hand, reveals a clear dependence on France, for the double dome, and the arrangement above the inner dome, connecting it with the lantern at the top, are extremely close to Lemercier's dome of the Sorbonne.

Ill. 24

The drawings which Wren presented with his memorandum are exceptionally attractive, and are beyond question his own, the section being signed high up on the left between the two domes. They are pen drawings in pale brown ink, the roofs being washed with blue. Apart from their interest as designs, they are of considerable importance as standards of Wren's own draughtsmanship. More than nine hundred drawings connected with Wren's buildings are known, the largest collection being at All Souls College, Oxford, though the libraries of St Paul's Cathedral and of the Royal Institute of British Architects also own important examples. Naturally, many of them were drawn by assistants, but some of the finest are by Wren himself, and show that he enjoyed throughout his life the making of architectural drawings, and that he retained his precision of hand until he was over seventy.

In August 1666 the Commission were still discussing what should be done, and on the 27th John Evelyn reports in his *Diary* that Wren's scheme after much opposition was adopted. Within a week it was rendered useless, for on 2 September the Great Fire broke out. For three days it ravaged the City. The next day Evelyn noted: 'I left it this afternoone burning, a resemblance of Sodome, or the last day: . . . the ruines resembling the picture of *Troy*: *London* was, but is no more. . . .' And on the 4th he recorded its extension westward: 'the stones of Paules flew like grenados, the Lead melting down the streetes in a streame, and the very pavements of them glowing with fiery rednesse, so as nor horse nor man was able to tread on them'. It was a calamity of the first order, for about seven-eighths of the City was destroyed, only a small section on the east side, near the Tower of London, having escaped. The area covered by the City of London (the title is still retained) was *Ill. 26* relatively small, lying on the north side of the Thames east and west of London Bridge, but it was the centre of great commercial activity, and was densely populated for the citizens lived where they worked. It was not the centre of the government of England, for that was based upstream in the City of Westminster, which contained the old Palace of Westminster then used by Parliament, the Abbey, and the King's palaces of Whitehall and St James's. The two cities were joined by the Strand and Fleet Street, with a small area of buildings to the north. The Great Fire, fanned by a strong east wind, spread west to the edge of the City of Westminster, for much of the Temple, south of Fleet Street, was destroyed, and it might have spread further had not the King been personally active in the blowing-up of buildings, thus leaving clear spaces across which the fire could not leap.

The problem of rebuilding was formidable. Many hundreds of houses had been burnt, and with them the title-deeds defining the properties; more than eighty churches were destroyed or seriously damaged; and the greater part of the Cathedral was in ruins.

A Commission to deal with the position was quickly appointed, consisting of three men nominated by the King, of whom Wren was one, and three appointed by the City. Two of the latter were experienced builders, and the third was Dr Robert Hooke, Professor of Mathematics at Gresham College, and a close friend of Wren's. Even before the Commission had met, plans for the new City were proposed by four of the members. Of those which have survived, there is no doubt that Wren's was by far the most imaginative. It was indeed a remarkable feat, for he produced it by 11 September, going himself to inspect the destruction. Instead of the tangle of narrow and often twisting streets which were the legacy of the Middle Ages, he proposed an ordered city with streets of three different widths. A civic centre (where the Royal Exchange now stands) was to be surrounded by buildings for the Mint, the Post Office, the Excise Office and 'Ensurances'. From it, streets were to radiate, one of the most important running west to St Paul's, which again was to stand in an open space. Further but smaller spaces with streets radiating from them were also proposed. Vistas were planned from space to space, churches were to stand on important corner sites, and an embankment was to be built along the river. Such ordered, large-scale

Ill. 27

26 Leake's engraving of the survey of the ruins of the City of London, 1666. The medieval City was within the old walls, the gates of which remained, but by 1666 the jurisdiction of the Lord Mayor had been extended to the west beyond the Fleet River which appears running south into the Thames

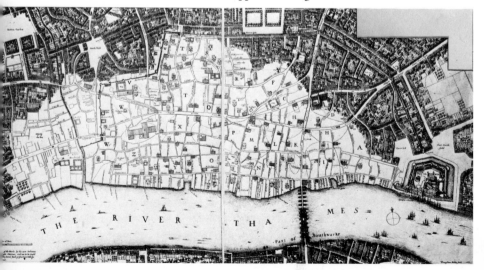

27 Wren's plan for the City of London, 1666

planning was totally new in England, but the conception of radiating streets and vistas goes back to Sixtus V's work in Rome, with its long streets radiating from the Piazza del Popolo, and Wren would have seen something of such planning when he was in Paris, above all in Henri IV's scheme for the Place de France, which, though not completed, was accessible *Ill. 28* in engravings.

28 Châtillon's engraving of the Place de France, Paris

Had Wren's plan been carried out, London would have become a beautiful city. But the position was too urgent for the delay which must have been caused by redistributing old sites for new purposes; and the citizens forestalled the Commission by going back and rebuilding on their old foundations. All the Commission achieved was a Rebuilding Act of 1667, under which timber houses and over-hanging upper storeys were forbidden, and the danger of fire therefore lessened. A standard of height was also set, which varied according to the importance of the streets. Finally, the Act put a tax on all coal coming into the Port of London (known as 'sea-coal', though it was shipped from the north of England), which was to compensate owners whose sites were taken for such improvements as could be made and also to finance the cost of public buildings. The relation of this tax to Wren's future work will appear in later chapters.

The last years of the decade mark the final emergence of Wren as a professional architect, though he did not resign from his Chair of Astronomy at Oxford till 1673, and his interest in the Royal Society and its scientific pursuits remained for the rest of his life.

Ill. 29 Two pieces of work outside London during these years are of some interest. The Chapel of Emmanuel College, Cambridge, was begun in 1668, though the design dates from at least the previous year, when a model in wood was sent down to the College. It shows Wren, for the first time, using related blocks instead of the single elements of Pembroke College Chapel and the Sheldonian Theatre. The high centrepiece is an exercise on the antique temple-front theme, for it has a giant order carrying a pediment, the latter broken in the centre by a block which is the base of a small domed lantern. On each side are lower wings set on arcades which carry through the design of the lower part of the centrepiece. The general composition may have been suggested by the Chapel of Peterhouse built by Wren's uncle Matthew and consecrated in 1632, but there the detail is still Late Gothic, whereas Wren's design is an interesting

29 Emmanuel College, Cambridge. Chapel range

if not entirely successful attempt to clothe it in classical dress. The three sections of the design have separate roofs, suggesting French influence, and though the centrepiece has some dignity, both the handling of the detail and the integration of the parts reveal a certain immaturity. Moreover, the façade is not in fact the front of the Chapel, which lies back from it behind the Master's Gallery.

In the same year Wren was consulted by his friend Dr Seth Ward, now Bishop of Salisbury, about the state of his Cathedral. Since Ward had been one of Wren's teachers at Oxford, and his predecessor in the Chair of Astronomy, he was fully aware of the younger man's qualities as a mathematician. Wren's report reveals a wonderfully thorough inspection of the fabric, and a consequent understanding of the achievements as well as the weaknesses of the medieval builders. He recommends immediate strengthening, especially to the spire and its supports. But he is not ashamed to admire the proportions and character of the building, chiefly on the grounds of its simplicity, its balance between richness of mouldings and 'large planes without an affectation of filling every corner with ornaments', and above all for its avoidance of elaborate window tracery: 'our Artist knew better that nothing could adde beauty to light'. This last sentence has a special significance. In the seventeenth century the study of light was a passionate interest of both scientists and artists. Wren is surely speaking here as an artist, and revealing himself as within the main stream of European tradition. This admiration for clear light falling on contrasted surfaces should not be forgotten, for it was to be an important formative influence on his style, above all in ecclesiastical building.

The only London building with which Wren was concerned in these years (beyond St Paul's Cathedral, to be discussed in *Ill. 30* Chapter V) was the new Customs House, erected in 1669. The design was probably his, though it appears to have been carried out by the Office of Works, and both the Surveyor, Sir John Denham, and the Comptroller, Hugh May, were also concerned with it. It was destroyed by fire in the early eighteenth century, and is known only from engravings, no original drawings having survived. It appears to have been Dutch rather than French in derivation, perhaps owing to the influence of Hugh May. As in most of Wren's early buildings, the handling and proportion of the orders, here Tuscan and Ionic, appears to be rather fumbling, but this and the awkward balance between voids and solids may well have been exaggerated by the engraver.

By the end of the decade Wren's position was completely changed. Up till now he had been a distinguished amateur, consulted by many, and especially by the King, largely on his reputation as a mathematician, though after his journey to France his increasing interest in architecture must have been widely known. In 1669 he became the chief architect to the Crown. The health of Sir John Denham, the Surveyor, had been in a poor state for some time, but when he died in March 1669 it was thought that John Webb, who had at one time acted as Deputy-Surveyor, and who had been promised the reversion, or Hugh May, would succeed him. Instead the King appointed Wren. Webb was offered the Deputy-Surveyorship, but wrote a not undignified letter, saying he would have been willing to

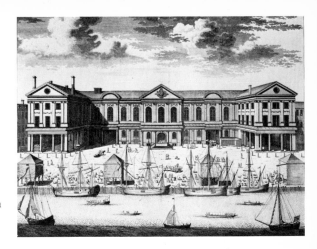

30 Customs House, London

serve jointly with the younger man, but could not serve under him. He soon retired to the country, and died in 1672. May was compensated by a rise in salary, and various jobs were found for him during the next few years, the most important being the Comptrollership of the Works at Windsor Castle in 1673. Work at Windsor Castle was not at this time automatically carried out by the main Office of Works in Whitehall, and May was to be responsible for extensive rebuilding there before his death in 1684.

The Office of Works, of which Wren now became head, consisted of the Surveyor and the Comptroller (Hugh May) and the King's Artisans – the Master Mason, the Master Carpenter, the Sergeant Plumber, with joiners, carvers, brick-layers and many others. There was also a Paymaster, a Clerk Engrosser, and a Purveyor who bought materials, while the main royal residences each had also their own Clerk of the Works. The office under Wren's control was therefore a large one, and since almost all the accounts have survived in the Public Record Office (many of them being printed in the volumes of the *Wren Society*), it is possible to follow, in some detail, the course of its many undertakings. It was responsible for the upkeep or alteration of all royal buildings and also for such temporary arrangements as might be required for State functions. It was not, however, responsible for anything but

43

royal works, though inevitably the Surveyor was likely to be consulted on other matters.

The post carried a house in New Scotland Yard, Whitehall, which then lay nearer Charing Cross than the present building of that name, and at the end of 1669 Christopher Wren married Faith, daughter of Sir Thomas Coghill of Bletchingdon near Oxford. They had probably known each other from childhood. The marriage appears to have been a happy one, though it was of short duration, for Faith died of smallpox in 1675, leaving one son, the younger Christopher, who was only seven months old. In 1677 Wren married for the second time, his wife being Jane Fitzwilliam, sister of Lord Fitzwilliam of Lifford. She died in 1680, leaving two children, Jane, said to be her father's favourite child, and William, who appears to have been delicate.

The other biographical event of note in Wren's life was the knighthood conferred on him by the King in 1673. It may well *Ill. 31* have been on this occasion that the fine bust, now in the Ashmolean Museum, Oxford, was made by Edward Pierce. It was presented to the University by the younger Christopher, who stated it had been made in 1673. It is an exceptionally fine example of English sculpture, but it is also fine in its suggestion of character, for it reveals both Wren's intelligence and his humanity.

31 Edward Pierce.
Marble bust of
Sir Christopher Wren

CHAPTER THREE

The City churches

In 1670 a second Rebuilding Act was passed by Parliament, under which the tax on coal shipped to London was increased. The larger part of this was now to go to the rebuilding of the City churches, while such money as could be spared was to be devoted to St Paul's Cathedral. A small committee was set up which was to be responsible for the churches. Wren, now Surveyor-General, was the chief member, but he was to be assisted by Dr Robert Hooke and Edward Woodroffe, a surveyor who had been working with Wren from 1668 and before that had been Surveyor to the Dean and Chapter of Westminster.

Eighty-seven churches, many of them very small, had been destroyed or damaged. It was decided that some parishes could conveniently be amalgamated, and fifty-two were therefore rebuilt. The fabric was to be paid for out of public funds, but the fittings were the responsibility of the parishes. In a number of cases all, or part of these were given by individuals or by bodies such as the City Companies. In addition, important churches, St Clement Danes and St James's, Piccadilly, and St Anne's, Soho, were built to the west of the City area.

Work was begun very quickly. Sixteen were put in hand in 1670, four more in 1671, and another fifteen before the end of the decade. The remainder date from the 1680s.

It is likely that in all cases Wren was responsible for the plan, and in many cases for much more, but the enormous amount of work that was on his hands makes it improbable that he supervised every detail. A number of the remaining drawings are in his hand, a few are by Dr Robert Hooke, and Hooke's *Diary* records constant meetings of both men on the various sites. Woodroffe's work cannot be separated, but it was probably measuring and supervising rather than designing, and he died in 1675 before much was completed. In some cases the detail on the building is coarse, and may well have been left to the craftsmen who were carrying it out; indeed, in the description of the churches given in *Parentalia*, the younger Christopher Wren states in one case that the 'Order is the workmen's own invention'.

Nevertheless, the City churches as a whole must be regarded as a very important part of Wren's early work. That they were always regarded as his creations is indicated by John Evelyn who, on 5 May 1681, notes in his *Diary* that Wren dined with him, and was building St Paul's and 'was in hand with the building of 50 Parish Churches: a wonderful genius had this incomparable person'. Unfortunately, it is more difficult to obtain a clear picture of Wren's intentions in the churches as they are now than in any other section of his work. Some were altered in the eighteenth century, but many more were mal-treated in the nineteenth. Interiors were rearranged or partly rebuilt, the high pews were replaced by chairs or benches, windows were altered and, worse still, were filled with Victorian stained glass. And interiors were often painted in heavy colours. It appears from the original building accounts, many of which remain, that the interiors were not coloured. There are payments for 'whiting' – i.e. whitewashing – or for painting in 'stone colour', and occasionally for painting in 'wainscot' – i.e. wood-colour – but nothing else except gilding. No stained glass was added, and if Wren's analysis of Salisbury Cathedral is recalled, it is evident that he would not have wished for it. Indeed, his aim in the churches appears to have been to re-create something of the effect of a light interior, with both plain and enriched surfaces, which he had admired at Salisbury in 1668.

Up to the Second World War, the great majority of the churches remained, and were still in use. Seventeen of them had already disappeared, having in most cases been demolished to make room for street improvements though some of them were adequately recorded before destruction. During the nineteenth century the character of the City had changed. Men no longer lived at their places of business, but had moved out to the new suburbs – in fact the age of commuters had begun, and before the war the chief use of the churches was for midday services or for concerts. But they suffered very heavily during the war, mainly from the raids with incendiary bombs in 1940 and 1941. Very few escaped damage, and some were totally destroyed. With the exception, perhaps, of Coventry Cathedral, it is not too much to say that they were the heaviest architectural loss sustained by Great Britain. A number of them have now been rebuilt, but they are often intended for special purposes, and so the interior arrangement has been changed. Moreover, much of the fine woodwork of Wren's day was burnt. Others will not be restored, though in some cases the tower is still standing.

The interest of the churches lies in two main aspects – the variety of their planning and interior design, and the beauty of their steeples. Exterior design is of far less importance than in seventeenth-century churches on the Continent, for very few of Wren's churches had any real façade to the street. The medieval churches which they replaced had often been almost completely surrounded by houses, and these houses had already been rebuilt. In one way it was an advantage that grand façades were not needed, for the work was urgent, money was limited and a simple exterior of brick with stone dressings, largely hidden from view, was both cheaper and quicker to build.

The remarkable variety in planning arises partly from the shape of the different sites, but must also be due to the ingenuity and experimental nature of Wren's mind, which led him to solve basically similar problems in a number of different ways. The primary problem was to provide churches which were suitable for Protestant worship designed in the idiom of classical architecture acceptable to the seventeenth century. Except for Inigo Jones's church of St Paul's, Covent Garden, in which the *Ill. 4*

47

chief emphasis is placed on the temple-like portico to the street, there was no precedent in England for such buildings, and Wren had, as it were, to provide his own vocabulary. We have some indication of the lines along which he thought, for much later in his life, an Act of Parliament was passed in 1708 for new churches to be built both east and west of the City, and Wren was appointed one of the Commissioners. He was by then too old to take an active part in their design, but he left a memorandum, written perhaps in 1711, summarizing his views in the light of his long experience.

Churches, he advised, should be as large as possible; 'but still, in our reformed Religion, it should seem vain to make a Parish church larger, than that all who are present can both hear and see. The Romanists, indeed, may build larger Churches, it is enough if they hear the murmur of the Mass, and see the Elevation of the Host, but ours are to be fitted for Auditories. I can hardly think it practicable to make a single Room so capacious, with Pews and Galleries, as to hold above 2000 Persons, and all to hear the Service, and both to hear distinctly, and see the Preacher.' Exposition, rather than the mysteries of religion, was the major concern of the Anglican Church. The building therefore should not be planned with the altar as the main focal point. The seats of the clergy reading the service, the lectern, and above all the pulpit must be so placed that every member of the congregation could see and hear. A very brief reading of the *Diaries* of John Evelyn or Samuel Pepys gives strong and contemporary support to Wren's emphasis on the importance of preaching. Sunday after Sunday they note the Biblical text on which the sermon was based, criticizing or praising the preacher's dissertation, and they grumble if they cannot hear. Wren's pulpits were carefully placed, and almost all of them had large sounding-boards above them, to help spread the sound of the voice.

The Counter-Reformation churches Wren had seen in Paris were naturally of no use to him as patterns, for though in a Jesuit church preaching was of importance, the main emphasis

48

was inevitably on the altar. In such churches, it was usually set in an apse, and the seats of the clergy were sharply divided from those of the congregation. In every church except St Clement Danes, which had an unusual site, Wren placed his altar against the flat east wall. Neither it, nor the seats for the clergy close to it, were divided off from the congregation except by altar rails, or raised above the main floor by a flight of steps. Even so, it must always be remembered that Anglicans, unlike more extreme Protestants such as Lutherans and Calvinists, considered an altar an essential element in a church, and its position is a crucial feature of all Wren's ecclesiastical designs.

With these conditions in his mind, Wren evolved a number of different types of building. Occasionally it is possible to find links with Holland, but on the whole the designs seem to have grown out of the sites. Generally speaking, the area covered by each new church was that of the medieval building it replaced; *Ills. 32–40* indeed, for reasons of both speed and economy, the old foundations were often used. Many of the sites were irregular in shape, perhaps because of additions to the old church after it was built or because of the angle of the streets which surrounded it. But Wren was prepared to ignore such difficulties. On the other hand, while many of his solutions appear to have grown out of local conditions, there is little doubt that, during the busy years of the 1670s, he greatly widened his knowledge of architectural style. Part of this would have been gained through his close association with Dr Robert Hooke. The *Diary* of the latter, covering the years 1672–80, is tedious reading, for much is taken up with Hooke's bodily ills, but it is useful in showing that he was a great buyer of architectural books and engravings – Italian, French, Dutch and Flemish. And whatever Hooke bought or borrowed, Wren must surely have seen.

Something is known of the library Wren himself left at his death, and this will be discussed in Chapter VIII, but it provides no information about dates of purchase. Wren may well have known books before he bought them. This is certain in the case of Vitruvius' treatise. He owned a copy of the Perrault

49

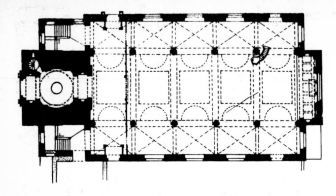

32 St Bride, Fleet
Street. Plan

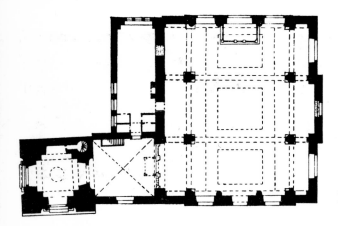

33 St Mary-le-Bow.
Plan

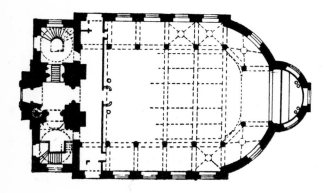

34 St Clement Danes.
Plan

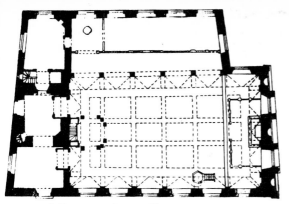

35 St Lawrence, Jewry. Plan

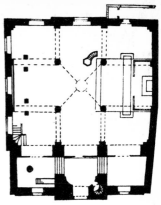

36 St Martin, Ludgate. Plan

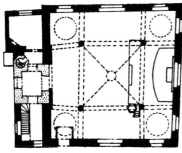

37 St Anne and St Agnes, Gresham Street. Plan

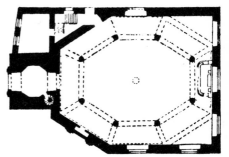

38 St Antholin, Watling Street. Plan

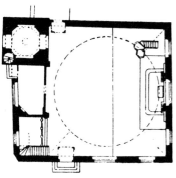

39 St Mary Abchurch. Plan

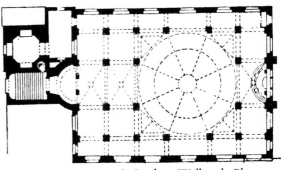

40 St Stephen, Walbrook. Plan

41 St Bride, Fleet Street. Interior before the Second World War. In the rebuilding the galleries have not been replaced, and the seating has been completely altered

edition of 1684. But among the accounts of the City churches now in the Bodleian Library at Oxford there is a payment, probably in September 1676, of £3 to his clerk, Andrew Phillips, for buying a copy of Vitruvius 'for the use of the office'. This may have been the earlier edition (1673) of Perrault's translation, but it is more likely to be the Latin edition of Daniele Barbaro. Hooke had bought a copy of the latter for the same sum in 1675, and apparently had a scheme, which came to nothing, of translating it.

Wren's churches fall into two main groups: fairly large oblong buildings, divided into the traditional nave and aisles, and smaller buildings, often almost square, but treated in a variety of different ways. The latter are perhaps the more ingenious, but it is surprising how greatly the larger churches *Ills. 32, 41* differ in their internal effect. In St Bride, Fleet Street, one of the churches begun in 1670, nave and aisles were divided by arcades

42 St Mary-le-Bow. Interior before the Second World War. The arrangement of the interior has been altered in the rebuilding

carried by large coupled columns, set on high bases. The nave
had a plastered barrel-vault, with oval clerestory windows
cutting into its surface, and the aisles had cross-vaults. But since
this was a church to be used by a large congregation, Wren
arranged galleries above the aisles, which combined a little
awkwardly with the giant columns. It is probable, however,
that the whole design of this church owes much to a classical
source. Vitruvius includes in his book a somewhat confused
account of a basilica he had built at Fano, and the plate which
accompanies it in Claude Perrault's edition of 1673 has a considerable similarity in the design of the roof and its supports,
and also in the placing of the gallery, to that of St Bride's. Moreover, as has been noted by Sir John Summerson, the Vitruvian
basilica had five bays, and a similar number occur in all Wren's
larger churches. On the other hand, Wren's use of galleries to
provide extra seating for the congregation need not necessarily
have a Vitruvian origin, for he would have seen them in use in
the French Huguenot church, the Temple at Charenton. *Ill. 22*

St Mary-le-Bow, also begun in 1670, has a different classical *Ills. 33, 42*
source. The plan is a curious one, largely dictated by the site,
for the tower alone has a frontage on to Cheapside; the visitor
entered under the tower, and had to turn left to face the east
end. The wide church had three bays only, nave and aisles being

43 St James, Garlickhythe

44 Christ Church, Newgate Street. Interior
before the Second World War

separated by piers with half-columns in front, a disposition, according to *Parentalia*, taken from the Basilica of Maxentius in Rome, then known as the Temple of Peace.

St James, Garlickhythe, a slightly later church begun in 1676, *Ill. 43* has single Ionic columns dividing nave and aisles. The aisles have flat ceilings, while above the columns in the nave are clerestory windows, which cut into the coving which runs up to the large flat panel, adorned with gilding, in the centre of the roof. Since this church has no coloured glass, and much of the original woodwork remains, it represents Wren's intentions more closely than some of the better-known churches.

In 1677, at Christ Church, Newgate Street (destroyed in *Ill. 44* 1940), Wren devised an interior which revealed his increasing maturity, for it had a sense of space composition absent in the churches so far discussed. The interior columns were set on high wood bases which rose to gallery level (thus avoiding the awkward relation of columns and galleries in St Bride's). Above the deep galleries, used by the children of Christ's Hospital, were flat ceilings, while the nave had shallow cross-vaults,

which removed all difficulty over the insertion of clerestory windows. Moreover, the galleries seemed an integral part of the wide and spacious church, and not merely an addition for convenience, as in St Bride's.

The last important variant of the nave and aisles type can be seen in two of the churches outside the City, St Clement Danes, begun in 1680, and St James's, Piccadilly, begun in 1682. In both, galleries, supported on square wooden piers, run round three sides of the church. At gallery level an order of small Corinthian columns carry the barrel-vaulted roof. In St Clement Danes, the bays of the gallery have cross-vaults, while in St James's each bay has a small barrel-vault at right angles to the main vault of the nave. In both cases it is therefore possible to light the church with large windows behind the gallery. Wren himself regarded St James's as a successful solution to the problem of church-building, for he commended it in his Memorandum after the Act of 1708, saying it was capacious, cheap to build, and also beautiful and convenient. Both these churches had fine fittings. At St James's the reredos

Ills. 34, 46

Ill. 45

45 St James's, Piccadilly

46 St Clement Danes.
Interior since rebuilding

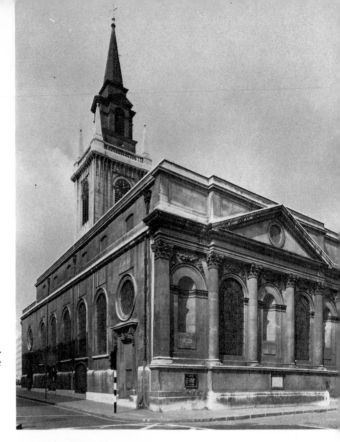

47 St Lawrence, Jewry.
East façade

48 St Lawrence, Jewry.
Interior since rebuilding

and font by Grinling Gibbons fortunately escaped the damage suffered by the building in 1941, as did the seventeenth-century organ case which had been made for Whitehall Palace. St Clement Danes, Wren's only apsed church, was burnt out, and the exceptionally rich plaster-work at the east end was destroyed.

Not all the large and important churches were divided into nave and aisles. St Lawrence, Jewry, begun in 1671, close to the Guildhall, was the church of the Corporation of London. Since the site is open to the east, Wren took the opportunity of designing a stone façade, using a Corinthian order of four half-columns carrying a pediment, with pilasters at the angles. Below are five arches, two of them enclosing windows, and the other three niches. The order has the relatively unusual feature of swags of fruit and flowers at the level of the capital. The same feature appears on the most distinguished building Wren could see in London, Inigo Jones's Banqueting House at Whitehall, and may be a borrowing from it. Inside, St Lawrence has an aisle on the north only, which originally contained a gallery, and a flat coffered ceiling above a cove, the latter being cut into by clerestory windows.

St Benet, Paul's Wharf, begun in 1677, a much smaller church, also has one aisle only, but the chief interest of the building,

Ill. 47

Ills. 35, 48

Ill. 49

49 St Benet, Paul's Wharf

apart from good fittings, lies in the exterior design of brick with stone coigns and garlands above the windows. There is clearly Dutch influence here, but whether it came from Philip Vingboons' book, which Hooke had bought in 1674, or from some other source, is hard to say.

Some but not all of the larger churches have been described in detail, for the differences between them reveal the flexibility of Wren's mind, and his ready invention in dealing with problems which could have been solved in a more stereotyped manner. The smaller also are exceedingly varied. There are a number of single-span buildings which differ in the design of their roofs, and there is a small group covered by domes. These domes are, however, an integral part of the interior space composition rather than a feature of the exterior design. St *Ills. 39, 50* Mary Abchurch, begun in 1681, is almost square, and the circular base of the shallow dome is carried on cantilever arches *Ill. 51* springing from the walls. In St Mildred, Bread Street, begun in 1677, the site was longer than it was wide. To reduce it to a square, Wren arranged a piece of richly plastered barrel-vaulting at the east and west ends, and erected a dome on

pendentives over the central square. Unfortunately, this church, which was in good condition, with its original pews and fittings, was completely destroyed in 1941. At St Swithin, Cannon Street, begun in 1677 and also destroyed in 1941, an eight-sided instead of a circular dome covered the main body of the church. In two other churches, both demolished in the nineteenth century, St Benet Fink, begun in 1670, and St Antholin, *Ill. 38* begun in 1678, Wren arranged a centralized building on long sites. At St Benet the area, roughly elliptical, was reduced to a decagon, with an oval dome carried on six columns, while at St Antholin a long octagon was the base of the oval dome.

All these buildings reveal that Wren was deeply interested in the centralized type of church, to which so much attention had been paid in both Renaissance and Counter-Reformation Europe. His solutions so far described are relatively simple, and have little direct relation to those of any other country. There is, however, a small group of churches, St Mary at Hill (begun in 1670 but much altered in the eighteenth and nineteenth *Ills. 36,* centuries), St Anne and St Agnes, and St Martin, Ludgate (both *37, 52,* begun in 1677), which seem to have direct links with Holland. *53*

50 St Mary Abchurch.
Interior since
restoration

51 St Mildred,
Bread Street.
Interior before the
Second World War

52 St Anne and St Agnes,
Gresham Street. Interior before
the Second World War and
subsequent alteration. The
church has been rebuilt but
simplified

In each case the main body of the church is roughly square, and
an inner square in the centre of the building is defined by four
columns. The ceiling in the four corners, outside the central
square, is low and flat, while four sections of higher barrel-
vaults run from the outer walls towards the centre between the
low ceilings. At St Anne and St Agnes, and at St Martin, the
barrel-vaults run into the central square and intersect, thus
making a cross-vaulted bay in the centre of the church; the
whole design can be read as a cross-in-square type. St Mary at
Hill, which in spite of alterations retains remarkably fine

53 St Martin,
Ludgate

fittings, has a low dome on pendentives instead of the cross-vault over the central bay. This pattern, with the low corners and the cross-vaulted centre, had already appeared in Holland. The first and most famous example was the Nieuwe Kerk at *Ill. 54* Haarlem, built by Jacob van Campen between 1645 and 1649, but the type was used elsewhere, for instance in the OosterKerk at Amsterdam of 1669–71. The similarity is so great that there must be a connection between the Dutch and English work, though it is not possible to say how Wren knew of the pattern. It may well have been through a verbal description or a drawing or even a picture. If so, his attention may very likely have been called to it by Dr Robert Hooke, for Hooke was certainly interested in Dutch architecture. His own independent works, such as the Royal College of Physicians (1672–78) or Bedlam Hospital, Moorfields (1675–76), both now destroyed, reveal *Ill. 55*

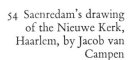

54 Saenredam's drawing of the Nieuwe Kerk, Haarlem, by Jacob van Campen

55 Robert Hooke. Bedlam Hospital, Moorfields

strong Dutch influence. Among his drawings in the British Museum is one of the Nieuwe Kerk, The Hague, probably copied from an engraving or another man's drawing. And his *Diary* records that in July 1674 Mr Story returned from Holland and told him of the new Lutheran Church at Amsterdam (probably the OosterKerk) and of the new Synagogue in the same town. 'Mr Story' was almost certainly Abraham Story or Storey, a mason who worked under Hooke at the Royal College of Physicians, and was also employed on two of the City churches, St Edmund King and Martyr (1670–79) and St Peter, Cornhill (1677–81). The former is the only example where a drawing can confidently be ascribed to Hooke, and the design is strongly Dutch in character. None of this is necessarily relevant to the cross-in-square plan, first used at St Mary at Hill which was begun in 1670, but it seems worth quoting as an indication of the way in which knowledge of buildings was carried, and this journey of Mr Story's may not have been the only one that was made. Moreover, Hooke's *Diary* does not begin until 1672.

Ills. 40, 56   The most complex, and by far the most accomplished, of Wren's centralized churches, St Stephen, Walbrook (1672–79), combines a cross-in-square plan with a large central dome. The site is in fact oblong, but by making one bay at the west into a miniature nave, Wren brings the central space to a square. The four corners of the building have the flat ceilings of the St Anne and St Agnes group, with vaults between them running inwards. It would have been possible for Wren to follow the pattern of many Continental churches and bring the square to a circle by erecting a dome on pendentives above the four arches made by the ends of the vaults. Instead he used a more complex pattern, for the dome rests on eight equal arches, carried on twelve columns. As will be seen in the chapters on St Paul's Cathedral, the idea of a dome on eight equal arches was in Wren's mind about 1673, and for many years to come. The use of this device at St Stephen's enabled him to bring more light into the church, for he inserted windows above his flat

ceilings, covering the space between them with small sections of groined vaults, which in fact help to support the dome. The windows on the east wall are large, but those on the side walls are relatively small ovals, and the upper windows play a great part in lighting the church. Indeed, before the recent insertion of stained glass, this building might well have shown how, in a classical idiom, Wren achieved something of the quality he had admired in Salisbury Cathedral. Even now, the first impact of the interior, which is reached by ascending a rather dark flight of steps, is considerable. In order to support his complex roof, Wren required sixteen columns (including those of the nave) and their grouping, together with the contrast of their plain shafts with the rich and slightly coarse plaster-work above, has a variety and interest far beyond that of any of the other churches. But the effect is largely intellectual and not emotional, and so the church is an exercise in the classical rather than in the Baroque. The rich fittings, which were given by the Grocers' Company, fortunately survived the damage to the church in 1940. They were not designed by Wren, for drawings showing 'offers' for them by different craftsmen survive in the Guildhall Library. Presumably, however, he gave some indication of what he thought was needed. The only considerable change in the interior is the replacement of the old high pews by benches. The pews reached to the top of the pedestals of the columns, and so would have made a dark mass with the columns rising above them, and the contrast between the lower and the upper part of the interior would have been stronger than it is today.

The variety of the interiors is matched, and indeed exceeded, by the variety of the steeples. In the Memorandum already referred to, written perhaps in 1711, Wren indicates the reason for their importance. Speaking of exterior design, he says: 'Such fronts as shall happen to lie most open in view should be adorned with Porticos, both for Beauty and Convenience; which together with handsome spires, or Lanterns, rising in good Proportion above the neighbouring Houses (of which I have given several Examples in the City of different Forms) may be of sufficient ornament to the Town, without a great expence for enriching the outward Walls of the Churches, in which Plainness and Duration ought principally, if not wholly, to be studied.' Wren had had no opportunity of building a portico, though he had hoped to add one to St Stephen, Walbrook, but that his steeples were indeed an 'ornament to the Town' is proved by many views showing the skyline of London. They evidently made a great impression on the Venetian painter, Canaletto, who visited London in 1746. He painted several *Ill. 57* views of the river, all showing a forest of steeples standing sharply against the sky, and in their slenderness making a striking contrast to the great mass of St Paul's.

Wren's steeples, which are varied in material as well as in form, some being in stone and others in lead, are often considerably later than the church to which they belong. The main work of building was largely finished by about 1685, but many of the steeples are fifteen or twenty years later. By then London was again prosperous, and money was forthcoming, so that the churches could be 'beautified'. They therefore show Wren's style at its most mature. A few, indeed, were not completed till Wren was over eighty, but the date of the designs cannot be deduced with certainty, and there is no evidence to suggest that they were the work of younger men.

One of the most famous is, however, early, for the building accounts of St Mary-le-Bow show that the steeple was built at *Ills. 58, 59* the same time as the church, and was finished in 1680. It is a remarkable creation, 225 feet high, and for nearly three hundred years it soared upward among the dense mass of surrounding buildings, and was indeed the only indication from Cheapside of the presence of the church. Since the Second World War the street has been widened and new buildings erected which do not crowd against the tower, and a small garden has been arranged at the west of the church. Similar alterations have been made round many of Wren's churches to the great advantage of the City, though this inevitably means that the churches can be seen from angles which Wren did not intend.

57 Canaletto. London and the Thames from Somerset House
Terrace looking towards the City

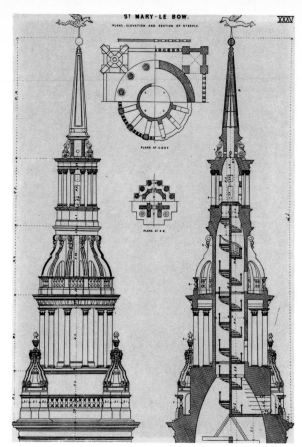

58 St Mary-le-Bow. Steeple   59 St Mary-le-Bow. Steeple and section

The steeple of St Mary-le-Bow, at the north-west corner of the church, starts as a square tower. The lowest storey has a *Ill. 60* dramatic door with a pair of Doric columns carrying an entablature, on which are seated two boys, the whole being set in a great niche with channelled voussoirs. The general idea is certainly borrowed from François Mansart's door for the *Ill. 61* Hôtel de Conti, but the proportions are changed, and the insertion of the Doric order gives it a new monumentality. The masons Thomas Cartwright and Colin Tompson were paid for

70

building 'ye Great Neech' in March 1672, and if Wren's
handling of detail here is compared with Emmanuel College, *Ill. 29*
Cambridge, of 1668, and still more with the Sheldonian Theatre *Ill. 13*
at Oxford of about 1664, it will at once be seen how much he
had already matured.

After a short plain section comes the belfry with a round-
headed window on each face and coupled Ionic pilasters at the
corners; and then the square tower ends with a balustrade. So
that the change from the square tower to the circular steeple is
not too marked, Wren has devised elaborate pieces of scroll-
work bearing urns, which carry the eye to the circular structure
above. The first storey of this is like a little temple surrounded by
a colonnade, with a balustrade above. Next is a curious feature
of twelve large inverted brackets round the central core. These
are in fact Wren's classical version of the 'bows' which gave the
church its name, for engravings made before the Great Fire
show that the tower was crowned by four Gothic half-arches
rising to a central pinnacle. After the circle of 'bows', St Mary's

60 St Mary-le-Bow. Doorway at base of tower
61 François Mansart's design for the doorway of the Hôtel de Conti, Paris

steeple narrows again, this time to a stepped square decorated by small Corinthian columns. From here, urns and brackets lead to a tall pyramid, which carries a ball and a weather-vane in the form of a dragon. It is evidence of Wren's care that in 1680 Edward Pierce, the mason and sculptor, not only made a wooden model of the dragon as a pattern for the bronze-caster, but also cut 'a relive in board to be profered up to discerne the right bignesse'.

The outside of the steeple is interesting enough, but a section shows that its construction was also complex. A conical dome in the belfry storey carries a very tall cylinder which rises to the level of the stepped square. This has a solid floor, while at the top it narrows again to a conical dome which carries the pyramid. But within the main cylinder a twisting wooden stair round a central newel rises from the belfry to the floor of the square.

Such a classical steeple of many storeys had never before been built in England, nor could Wren have seen one in France. Its origin is Italian, the best-known examples probably being the twin western towers of Antonio da Sangallo's model for St Peter's. These are probably derived from designs of Bramante, though the idea of the classical steeple had been voiced in Leon Battista Alberti's *De re aedificatoria*, first printed in 1485. Sangallo's model was engraved and it is possible that Wren knew the engraving. If he did not, it seems certain that it was known in the circle of Inigo Jones; for among John Webb's

Ill. 62

62 Sangallo's model for St Peter's, Rome

63 John Webb's design
for an ideal church

many drawings of ideal buildings, are several of churches with
many-storeyed classical steeples.   *Ill. 63*
  Wren's other many-storeyed steeples are all considerably
later than St Mary-le-Bow. They are less profuse in their
employment of differing motives for each exploits one main
idea. At St Bride, Fleet Street (1701–03), the steeple, which is   *Ill. 64*
some 10 feet higher than that of St Mary-le-Bow, appears at
first sight to be deceptively simple. The belfry storey is slightly
more massive, for instead of paired pilasters flanking the windows, it has pilasters with engaged columns at the angles, and a
segmental pediment on each face. The steeple proper consists
of four octagonal diminishing storeys, with an octagonal
pyramid above. The three lower storeys have the same design,
with pilasters at the angles, and the whole space between them
open, beneath a round-headed arch. The construction, however, is far more ingenious than that of St Mary-le-Bow, for
the centre of the steeple is not a cone, but an open stone staircase,
from which compartments radiate to the outer face.

Ill. 65 The steeple of Christ Church, Newgate Street (completed 1704), is a series of diminishing squares, the middle storey having an elegant free-standing Ionic colonnade, which gives it
Ill. 66 a curiously Neoclassical air. St Vedast, Foster Lane (1694–97), is perhaps the most Baroque of all Wren's steeples, for above the belfry the pilastered storeys are concave, convex and again
Ill. 67 concave. Such a design is reminiscent of Borromini, some of whose works would by now have been known to Wren in Falda's *Chiese di Roma*, but the treatment, with the delicate surface pattern made by the slightly projecting pilasters, is very different from the dramatic contrasts of light and shade contrived by the use of columns and broken entablatures in Italian Baroque architecture.

64 St Bride, Fleet
Street. Steeple

65 Christ Church,
Newgate Street.
Steeple

66 St Vedast, Foster
Lane. Steeple

67 Borromini. S. Ivo
della Sapienza, Rome

Another group, all late, and with small steeples above the
tower, does exploit the theme of grouped columns with entablatures broken forward above them, and so achieves a
strong contrast of light and shade and a variation of outline,
when viewed from different angles, which is closer in feeling
to Roman Baroque. St Michael, Paternoster Royal (completed
1713), has columns standing out from an octagonal core, with
vases above them, which add to the complexity of the silhouette.
St James, Garlickhythe (1714–17), varies the pattern by setting
paired columns on four of the eight faces, while St Stephen,
Walbrook, has three columns standing at the angles of a square
core. But as will be seen later, the grandest examples of this
group are the west towers of St Paul's Cathedral.

Ill. 68

Ill. 69

Ill. 70

Ill. 101

69 St James, Garlickhythe. Steeple

70 St Stephen, Walbrook. Steeple

For the tower and lantern of St Magnus Martyr (completed 1705) Wren seems to have turned to another source. Above the usual square belfry stage the form changes to an octagon, which carries a small lead cupola with a lead lantern and small spire above. Such a design, though treated with much less restraint, had been used earlier in the century at the Jesuit church at Antwerp, and among the drawings which have survived from

Ill. 71

Ill. 72

68 St Michael, Paternoster Royal. Steeple

Wren's office is one of the Flemish tower by an unknown hand. Wren's interest in such a tower with a small cupola dates, indeed, from much earlier in his life, for a drawing showing it exists for St Mary-le-Bow. That it is for that church is proved by the appearance of the great niched doorway to the tower; and so it must be before 1680. But a study of the drawings reveals that on more than one occasion Wren evolved a design which pleased him but which proved unsuitable for the immediate occasion. The design was laid aside but not forgotten, and used, probably with some variation, on a later building.

The high stone steeples are some of the best known of Wren's works, but the more modest designs in lead often have great charm. And, again, they are wonderfully varied in type. St Benet, Paul's Wharf (1677–83), has a small lead cupola carrying a lantern above the brick and stone tower. St Margaret, Lothbury (1686–90), has a slender obelisk over a small cupola. At St Nicholas, Cole Abbey (1671–77), the tower is capped by a cone, with a balcony at the top below small diminishing tiers giving rich changes of shape in contrast to the plain section beneath. But the finest of the lead steeples is that of St Martin, Ludgate (1677–84). The top storey of the stone tower is octagonal, and on it is set a small ogee dome in lead, with a balcony below the lantern, the whole rising to a tall and very slender obelisk and ball. There can be little doubt that Wren looked forward, when he was designing St Martin's, to the day when the top of Ludgate Hill would be crowned by the dome of St Paul's. This was not to be achieved until some twenty years later, but he foresaw the value of the contrast between the slender spire, and the grandeur of the west towers and soaring dome of St Paul's.

The lead spires, particularly those of St Martin, Ludgate, and St Nicholas, Cole Abbey, suggest links with Holland, though no very close prototypes exist, and by the time Wren was building them he could well have been capable of himself translating the medieval spire form into lead, with such additions as would render it classical.

Ill. 49

Ill. 73

78

71 St Magnus Martyr, London Bridge. Tower

72 Pieter Huyssens (?). St Charles Borromeo, Antwerp. Tower

73 St Martin, Ludgate. Steeple

Much space has been given to the City churches for they are of enormous importance in Wren's career. As has been shown, work on them began in 1670, when he still had had little experience in building. They must have taught him much, both about design and about practical problems of every kind, and the knowledge gained, especially in the early part of the 1670s, was invaluable when he came to tackle the far more complex problems of St Paul's. They were also a training-ground for the team of craftsmen who were to work for him for the rest of their lives. Names recur again and again in the building accounts of the churches – the masons Christopher Kempster, Thomas Cartwright, Samuel Fulkes and Edward Strong, the plasterers Henry Doogood and John Grove, and the carvers Edward Pierce (who was also a mason), William Emmett and Jonathan Maine. Almost all of them were to work on St Paul's. Though much of their work was destroyed in the Second World War, enough remains to assess its quality, and to enjoy the comfortable richness of Wren's interiors, so much less austere than the Calvinist churches of Holland and so unemotional compared with Italian or even Flemish Baroque.

Lastly, to the student of Wren's work the churches are specially revealing. They show the ingenuity and flexibility of his mind in dealing with many similar problems in a number of different ways. The rapid maturing of his style can also be followed in them; and though on occasion his solutions may appear a little dull, it must always be remembered that money was short, site conditions difficult, and the sheer mass of work made it inevitable that something had to be left to lesser men. The brilliance of St Stephen, Walbrook (1672–79) is a true indication of what he could do, and a fitting prelude to the building of St Paul's.

CHAPTER FOUR

The planning of St Paul's

Wren's fifty-two City churches, important though they may be, are only a small part of his work. Throughout the years when he was building them, he was constantly occupied with the problems of his greatest creation, St Paul's Cathedral, and at the same time was dealing with a number of important secular commissions. Few architects have carried out so much with such success.

Old St Paul's, about which Wren had advised in the summer of 1666, was not completely destroyed by the Great Fire. The choir was in ruins, but part of the old Romanesque nave, cased by Inigo Jones, was still standing, and Jones's great portico at the west end, though badly calcined, still remained. It was hoped at first that some use could be made of the old building, and in January 1668 the Commission for rebuilding the City ordered that a temporary choir, which would naturally contain both altar and pulpit, should be arranged at the west end. Four months later, however, Dean Sancroft wrote to Wren in Oxford that the third pillar from the west had fallen, revealing that Jones's casing of the exterior had not been properly keyed to the old wall. The Dean continued: 'In fine, it is the opinion of all men, that we can proceed no further at the West End. What we are to do next is the present deliberation, in which you are so absolutely and indispensably necessary to us, that we can do nothing, resolve on nothing, without you. . . . You will think fit, I know, to bring with you those excellent Draughts and Designes you formerly favoured us with.' From this time onwards Wren was personally responsible for the work at St Paul's, the commission being given to him by the Dean and Chapter, though the money for rebuilding had to be found by the government out of the tax on sea-coal.

Ill. 23

Ill. 74
Ill. 75

81

74 T. Wyck's drawing
of the ruins of Old
St Paul's

After Wren had reported in May that St Paul's was indeed in a completely ruinous state, a Royal Warrant was issued in July 1668 for the final demolition and clearing of the east end, the old choir and the central tower, 'in such a manner as shall be judged sufficient to make room for a new Choir of a faire and decent fabrick neare or upon the old foundations.' At the same time, the stone-work of the west end was to be taken down carefully in case it could be used again. The Dean appears to have been willing to accept the idea of a new choir only as a stage in the rebuilding, for he wrote asking Wren to come, 'that we may prepare something to be proposed to his Majesty (the Designe of such a Quire, at least, as may be a congruous Part of a greater and more magnificent work to follow).' He did not agree that no more could be done until money was found, when a final design could be made to fit the sum available, but stated, 'the way their Lordships [i.e. the Archbishop and Bishops concerned] resolve upon, is to frame a Design, handsome and noble, and suitable to all the Ends of it, and to the Reputation of the City, and the Nation, and to take it for granted, that Money will be had to accomplish it.'

The dual control under which Wren was to work was to bring some problems in reconciling the wishes of the clergy with the financial contribution of the government, but the

75 T. Wyck's drawing of the
   ruins of Old St Paul's

most urgent task was the clearing of the site. This was a most
formidable undertaking, especially as the lead from the roofs,
melted by the Great Fire, had run down the walls, and made
them much harder to demolish. Most of the work was done by
hand with pickaxes, while as many labourers as could be
employed on the crowded site shifted the debris away. It is not
surprising that the building accounts, which still exist, include
sums for the repair of wheelbarrows. Gunpowder was used to
blow up the remains of the central tower, but after an accident
it was considered too dangerous, and Wren finally had recourse
to a battering-ram, manned by thirty labourers. The task of
clearing was rendered more difficult by the state of the surrounding streets, which made it hard to get carts up the hill to
the Cathedral, but they were repaved by the end of the year,
and the rubble taken away to be used for levelling parts of the
City not yet restored. Inevitably accidents occurred, but the
Dean and Chapter were good employers, for they paid doctors'
bills, funeral expenses, and some compensation to widows;
but considering the extent and difficulty of the work, serious
accidents were few.

During 1669 an office for Wren and his assistants was set up
in the old Convocation House on the south side of the Cathedral
which had escaped serious damage. And there William Cleere,

Ill. 76
Ill. 77

a joiner and carver, made a wooden model of Wren's design for a new cathedral, payments to him in April and June of 1670 amounting to £200. This first design was for a curious and original building, relatively small in scale and perhaps planned with the knowledge that not much money was available. It consisted of two parts, a rectangular building to the east, and west of it a square section surmounted by a dome. The rectangle, which was intended for the services, was flanked by loggias on the ground storey, making the interior at this level somewhat narrow and dark, but at first-floor level it widened, with galleries over the space occupied by the loggias, lit by large round-headed windows. For the roofing Wren seems to have anticipated his arrangement at St James's, Piccadilly, for the building was covered by a barrel-vault carried on columns in front of the galleries, while each bay of the gallery had a small barrel-vault running out to the windows. The loggias were presumably intended to fulfil the same purpose as Inigo Jones's great west portico. In Shakespeare's time the nave of Old St Paul's was used by the citizens of London as a place of business, where servants could be hired or bargains made, and the portico had been built by the desire of King Charles I and Archbishop Laud, who were determined the desecration should cease. Wren's loggias were not porticoes with straight entablatures, but arcades set between Ionic columns, the pattern being repeated by the round-headed windows above, though in the upper storey the order is Corinthian. A battered fragment of the model for this part of the church still remains in the Model Room at St Paul's, and one drawing is known from which the arrangement and details can be reconstructed. Nothing, unfortunately, is known of the domed portion at the west. Hooke refers to it as a 'Library Body', but it may perhaps also have been intended to give additional space and splendour to services on State occasions.

The model seems to have met with some approval. It was carried to Whitehall, and had to be mended when it was brought back in June 1672; in November of that year Hooke

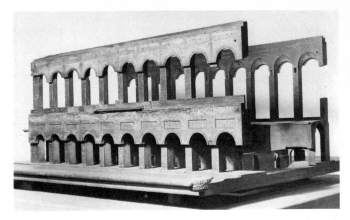

76 St Paul's Cathedral.
First Model

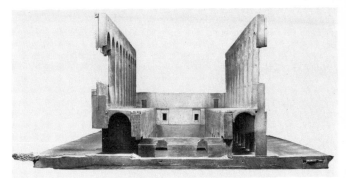

77 St Paul's Cathedral.
First Model

saw it approved by the King. It was not, however, universally admired. The only criticisms which are known today are those of Sir Roger Pratt, which may be slightly tinged with jealousy; for Pratt had been a member of the Pre-Fire Commission for the Repair of St Paul's, and he knew that he had travelled in Italy, and Wren had not. He saw the model in the Convocation House on 12 July 1673, and complained that it was unlike any cathedral in the world, that space was wasted on useless porticoes, and that the dome was at the west end and not over the centre of the church. He also disliked the darkness of the nave, and the fact that the building had ten windows each side, whereas architects usually preferred an uneven number. Some of these criticisms were justified, but the defence against them given in *Parentalia* is illuminating. It is true that this was written long

after the event, but it seems probable that the younger
Christopher was voicing the opinions of his father when he
wrote that the Surveyor had done what he was asked. He had
contrived 'a Fabrick of moderate Bulk but good Proportion;
a convenient Quire with a Vestibule, and Porticoes, and a
Dome conspicuous above the Houses'. It 'would have been
beautiful, and very fit for our Way of Worship; being also a
convenient Auditory. . . .'

   Others of more influence than Pratt disliked the First Model,
either (according to *Parentalia*) on the grounds that it deviated
too much from the traditional cathedral form, or that it was
not grand enough, and by the time Pratt voiced his opinions,
Wren had submitted further drawings to the King. In
November 1673, Charles II issued a long Commission for rebuilding the Cathedral. In it he speaks of the several designs
prepared by the Surveyor and specifies 'one of which We do
more especially approve, and have commanded a Model
thereof to be made in so large and exact a manner, that it may
remain as a perpetual and unchangeable rule and direction for
the conduct of the whole Work.' It goes on to appoint a large
number of Commissioners, both ecclesiastical and lay, to be
responsible for the undertaking, and also for the collection of

79 St Paul's Cathedral. Great Model, interior

money from private sources or from fines imposed by the
prerogative courts, and announces that the King will give
£1000 a year from the Privy Purse.

By the time the Commission was issued, the new model was
already under way. Since it was to be larger and far more
impressive than the First Model, considerable preparations had
to be made. During the months between April and September
1673, William Cleere the joiner was paid £42 2s. 6d. 'for a
Table and Frame for the intended new Model of the Church to
stand upon', and also for two tables on trestles for Wren and his
assistant Woodroffe to draw upon. On 22 September, John
Tillison, who had been Clerk of the Works to Old St Paul's,
reported to the Dean that Wren and Woodroffe had spent the
last week in the Convocation House 'drawing the Lines of ye
Designe of the church upon ye Table there, for ye Joyner's
Directions for making ye New Model'. In the next year Tillison
bought 70 yards of coarse calico at 7d. a yard 'for the Window

87

78 St Paul's Cathedral. Great Model

Curtains in the Convocation House to keep the heat of the sun from the Model'. It is not surprising that care was taken to preserve the new model, generally called the 'Great Model', for it cost over £500 to make and is a beautiful object. There are payments to twelve joiners, to Richard Clare (or Cleere), a carver, for cutting more than three hundred and fifty capitals, as well as flowers, festoons and cherubim's heads, to plasterers and to Robert Streeter, the Sergeant-Painter, for gilding. *Ills. 78, 79* Luckily it can still be studied in the Model Room at St Paul's. It is 18 feet long and is for a very large church, immeasurably grander than that of the First Model. In it, Wren displays to the full his growing knowledge of architecture.

Ill. 81 The plan was a complete novelty, for the building was in essence in the form of a Greek cross with four equal arms plus an extension to the west. The arms were joined by concave walls, and over the centre of the church was a dome carried on eight piers, with complete circulation round them at ground level. At the west, entered under a great Corinthian portico, was a vestibule covered by a smaller dome. The dimensions of the building would have been considerable, for the base of the dome would have been 120 feet, 8 feet wider than that finally executed, and only 17 feet smaller than St Peter's, Rome. A

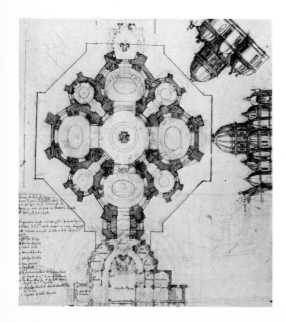

80 François Mansart's design for a Bourbon chapel, Saint-Denis

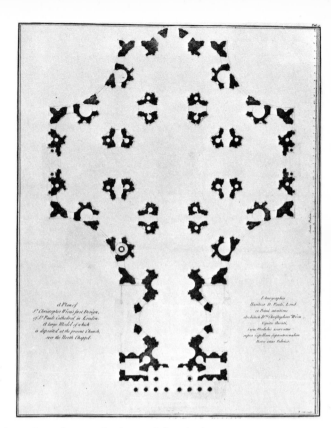

81 St Paul's Cathedral.
Great Model, plan

number of drawings showing the evolution of the design are at All Souls College, Oxford, all apparently made by Edward Woodroffe under Wren's direction. His draughtsmanship, firm and a little coarse compared with Wren's delicate penmanship is easy to identify, but he was to die in 1675, so none of the later drawings for St Paul's are his.

For this splendid design, said to be his favourite, Wren borrowed from a number of sources. The dome is Bramantesque in the even rhythm of the drum, but Michelangelesque in the ribbed section above it. The Corinthian portico is taken over from Inigo Jones, though a pediment is added, and the domed vestibule may echo Sangallo's design for St Peter's. The source of the arrangement of the dome, over eight instead of the more usual four arches, is probably François Mansart's abortive design   *Ill. 80*

89

for a Bourbon chapel to be added to Saint-Denis, which Wren would probably have known while he was in Paris, though in the drawing for this the central space is surrounded by chapels, and not by a continuous ambulatory as in the Great Model. It is just possible that one of Mansart's drawings for the chapel gave Wren the idea of joining the arms of the Greek cross by concave walls, for it shows the building on a base with sloping, though not concave, sides. No church Wren could have seen in France presents this feature, though there is a design for a palace which uses them in Antoine Le Pautre's *Œuvres d'Architecture* of 1652. On the other hand, among the Webb drawings of ideal

Ill. 82 churches is one for a Greek cross building, the arms of which are joined by convex walls. Details of the elevation (though not of the dome) are so close to those of the Great Model that it is conceivable that Wren used it as a pattern, but for greater elegance reversed the curve of the walls.

In spite of such borrowings, the Great Model is by no means a piece of arid eclecticism. It is an original, and indeed a noble design, fine in proportion and lucid in the relation of its parts. Compared with the great Baroque churches of the Continent, the handling may perhaps seem a little cold, but it must be remembered that some of the painted decoration still visible in the interior would have been carved in relief and so have given variation of surface; and judging from the executed building, the exterior would certainly have received more embellishment. It is indeed known that a series of small statues was made to stand on the parapet and so to break the skyline, but they have all now disappeared. Dr Robert Hooke, who saw them on 5 September 1674, says they were by a 'Dutchman'. This may well imply that they were the work of the famous Grinling Gibbons, who had been born in Rotterdam in 1648 of an English father and a Dutch mother. His early life was spent in Holland, but he was in England by 1671, when he was discovered by John Evelyn working in a hut at Deptford, and remained in England till his death in 1721, though he seems always to have been regarded as a foreigner, and his command of English was

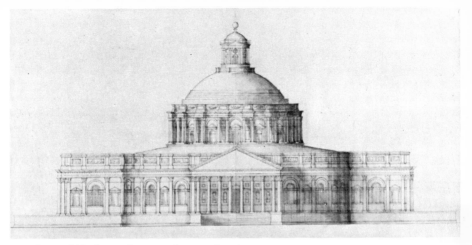

82 John Webb's design for a Greek cross church

limited. If these little figures were his work, it was the first occasion on which Wren employed him.

By the time Hooke saw the model, work was beginning on the digging of the foundations, a difficult task since the site was not yet cleared. But Wren was now to face a major disappointment, perhaps the greatest of his career. For though the Great Model, according to *Parentalia*, pleased 'Persons of Distinction, skill'd in Antiquity and Architecture', the clergy thought it unsuitable. To them, the essence of a cathedral lay in the traditional Latin cross form, in which daily services could be held in the choir, and those for a larger congregation could use the nave. The Anglican Church has at all times made much of continuity, holding that only errors had been abandoned at the Reformation. Just as the Apostolic tradition in the consecration of bishops had been conserved, so the cathedral form was a vital link with earlier Christianity. In a church built to the Great Model design, it would have been impossible to follow tradition by holding daily services in the choir, for such choir as there was lay only between the eastern apse and the area of the dome. Moreover, the final design implies that there was a further, practical reason combined with the clergy's objection, for the whole question of finance was still uncertain, and it was clearly more prudent to launch out on a building that could be completed and put into use in stages – the choir first, and then, as more money came in, to continue westward with the nave. The Great Model design did not lend itself to such treatment, for as soon as the eastern end was built, the piers of the dome would be reached, and all eight must be raised before the Cathedral could be roofed.

It is impossible to follow the exact sequence of events between the autumn of 1674 and the spring of 1675 in any contemporary documents. No correspondence between Wren and the clergy has survived and there may well have been none, since problems could be discussed verbally. And the accounts record only the progress of the long work of clearing the site. *Parentalia*'s summary is tantalizingly brief. It relates that 'the Surveyor resolved to make no more models, or publickly to expose his Drawings'; and that he 'turned his thoughts to a cathedral form (as they called it) but so rectified as to reconcile as near as possible the Gothick to a better manner of architecture; with a cupola and above that instead of a lantern a lofty spire and large porticoes.'

Wren's methods were so far effective that on 14 May 1675 a Royal Warrant was issued, approving designs still stitched to it in the Library of All Souls College, Oxford. Its wording is of interest in view of the long-drawn-out difficulties of the previous seven years. It states that the money now available, 'though not proportionable to the Greatness of the Work, is notwithstanding sufficient to begin the same', and should be enough to 'put a new Quire in great forwardness; and whereas among divers designs which have been presented to Us, We have particularly pitched upon one, as well because We found it very artificial [i.e. ingenious], proper, and useful; as because it was so ordered that it might be built and finished by Parts.' *Parentalia* adds: 'And the King was pleased to allow him [Wren] the liberty in the prosecution of his work, to make variations, rather ornamental than essential, as from time to time he should see proper.' The last sentence probably provides the key to the executed design of St Paul's, for it is hard to believe that Wren really intended to carry out the Warrant designs.

The Warrant design is to a great extent a compromise, for it gives the clergy what they wanted, but attempts to retain some features on which Wren's mind was set. The plan was a Latin cross, with a choir of three bays and a nave of five, all of which were to be covered by cross-vaults. At the east was an additional half-bay and a small apse. Transepts, each of three bays, were entered through inset porches, while at the west of the nave was a large projecting portico. At the crossing was a dome, carried as in the Great Model on eight piers. This plan, in contrast to that of the Great Model, would have lent itself to building by parts, for the choir could be finished and put into use before the rest of the church was begun. *Ill. 83*

The elevations show that the whole exterior design, except for the dome, follows very closely Inigo Jones's recasing of the nave, with its broad pilasters. The silhouette of the building, with the aisles lower than the nave or choir, also follows Jones, who had merely adapted the normal medieval arrangement, clothing it in classical dress. So far the designs were inoffensive, if somewhat tame. But the central feature is curiously bizarre. Rising over the centre of the church is a low, broad dome, set on rings of masonry like those at the bottom of Bramante's design for St Peter's. Above this is a tall Michelangelesque drum, its ancestry being clear in the coupled columns with scrolls above them. The drum carries a small ribbed dome, and the whole is surmounted by a tall steeple, at first sight not unlike that Wren was later to build at St Bride, Fleet Street, in six diminishing stages. The sectional drawing shows that the lower dome was open at the top, and that the centre was in fact covered by a semicircular dome above the top of the drum, while the steeple appears to be a timber construction. *Ill. 84* *Ill. 23* *Ill. 85* *Ill. 86*

The lower dome would hardly have been seen by a spectator standing on the ground outside the building, and so the central

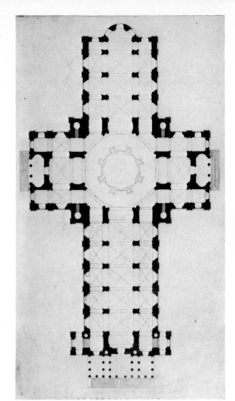

83 St Paul's Cathedral. Warrant
design, plan

84 St Paul's Cathedral. Warrant
design, south side

85 St Paul's Cathedral.
Warrant design, west end

86 St Paul's Cathedral.
Warrant design, sectional
drawing

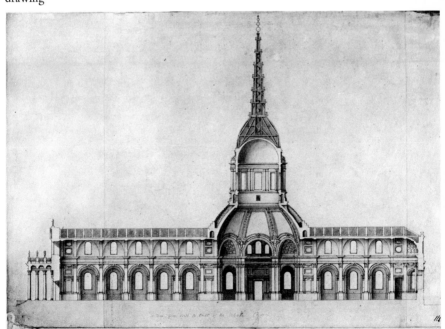

feature might have seemed slightly less grotesque than the drawings which are in true elevation, presupposing the eye is on every level. Nevertheless, it is almost impossible to believe that these drawings, which are in Wren's own hand, are later than the Great Model, for they are far more immature, above all in their sense of proportion. If they are earlier than the Model, they could, with their reliance on Inigo Jones, date from perhaps 1668, when the Dean asked Wren to bring drawings with him. There are also payments to Wren early in 1672, before the First Model was approved, for 'drawing several draughts of the church, and attendance severall times upon his Majesty concerning the affairs of the same.' It is conceivable that Wren, in his anxiety to get work started, produced existing drawings which he knew the clergy would approve, and that the King issued the Warrant with the knowledge that alterations which were not only 'ornamental' would quickly be made.

On 18 June 1675 contracts were signed with two masons for the beginning of work on the choir. The first, Joshua Marshall, was Master Mason to the Crown; the other, Thomas Strong, owned stone quarries near Oxford, and both were already working with Wren on the City churches. *Parentalia* records how, when they were setting out the site for the new building, Wren called to a labourer to bring him a stone to mark a certain point. One was picked up at random, and the Surveyor, when turning it over, saw it was part of an old tombstone, inscribed with the prophetic word: *Resurgam* (I shall arise again). The story of the incident must have come from Wren himself.

CHAPTER FIVE

The building of St Paul's

The foundation-stone of the new Cathedral was laid at the south-east corner of the building on 21 June 1675. Joshua Marshall was responsible for the work on the south side of the choir, while Thomas Strong built the east wall and the apse.

A comparison between the Warrant plan and the executed plan reveals that the masons must quickly have become aware, if indeed they did not know in advance, that major alterations were being made to the Warrant design. The outer walls are more than 2 feet thicker, the aisles are narrower and the shape of the piers dividing the choir and its aisles is changed. Moreover, as soon as the outer walls rose above ground level, changes in the design of the elevation would have been apparent. A row of small windows, lighting the crypt, were inserted in the base of the walls, and the clumsy broad pilaster-strips, taken over from Inigo Jones's recasing, were replaced by more elegant coupled pilasters. *Ill. 83*

Ill. 87

Ill. 89

As the building proceeded, the reason for the thickening of the walls would gradually have become apparent. They were indeed required to bear a much greater load than the walls in the Warrant plan. There the walls rose only to aisle level, above which the Cathedral was set back to the width of the choir, the upper storey with its round-headed clerestory windows being shorter than the lower. But the executed design shows two almost equal storeys, and both are in the same plane. The thickening of the walls was therefore necessary partly in order to carry the greater weight of the upper walls. The new design, with the wall rising unbroken from the ground to the great cornice, changed the whole character of the building, for it gave an impression of size and grandeur completely lacking in the Warrant design. It also presents one of the most remarkable *Ills. 84, 85*

Ill. 88

97

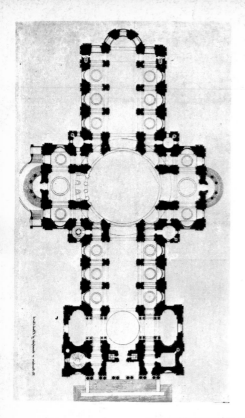

87 St Paul's Cathedral. Plan of cathedral as executed

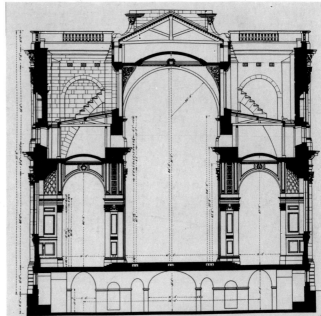

88 St Paul's Cathedral. Cross-section through choir

89 St Paul's Cathedral from the south-east

examples of Wren's ingenuity. The fact that the walls are in one plane suggests that the traditional arrangement of a cathedral, with choir or nave higher than the aisles, has been abandoned, and that the whole interior is the same height. This is not the case. The upper part of the wall is a false wall, the windows of the choir being set many feet behind it. And, behind the false wall, Wren has set flying buttresses, stretching above the aisle roofs to help support the vault of the choir. The false walls, with the wide space behind them, and the heads of the flying buttresses can best be seen in an air view of the Cathedral. And, though the effect of the false walls is to give grandeur to the elevation, their function is to control and remit thrusts, above all the enormous thrust of the dome. The dome was not to be completed for nearly forty years, and it is not possible to date with complete certainty any of the drawings which show variants of it, but the problem of its support was clearly in Wren's mind from the beginning of the building.

Ill. 90

Ill. 91

90 St Paul's Cathedral. Back of screen wall, showing buttresses above aisle roof

91 St Paul's Cathedral. Air view

It is hardly possible that even Wren, who was an exceptionally quick worker, could have evolved the new scheme between the issue of the Warrant on 14 May 1675, and the signing of the contracts with Marshall and Strong on 18 June. The changes must have been already in his mind, and in all probability already set down on paper. A few drawings remain which appear to suggest an early stage of the final design, but with a low dome. Another, which is in Wren's own hand, shows the building to cornice level as carried out, but with a large dome which is very close to Michelangelo, and west towers based on Bramante's design for the Tempietto at San Pietro in Montorio in Rome. Whether this dates from 1675, as has been suggested, or from rather later is impossible to determine, but at least it gives a clear idea of the change from the Warrant to the executed design.

Ill. 92

Ill. 84

Many new problems had now to be faced. The clearing of the site must be speeded up, and in October 1675 one hundred and twenty-four labourers were working at it. Seven hundred and fifty-three cartloads of rubbish had been carried away by January 1676, and the carting went on for many months more. The best of the stone from Jones's old west end and transept fronts had to be sorted out and put aside for re-use. Timber had to be brought and worked into scaffolding and centering for arches. Bricks as well as lime and sand for mortar had to be brought to the site, and by the middle of 1676 new stone was also needed. This required special organization, for the work of Inigo Jones, both at the Banqueting House at Whitehall and at St Paul's, had shown that stone from the Portland quarries in Dorset was the most durable in the damp, smoky London air. This had to be brought round to the Port of London by sea, unshipped below London Bridge, for its arches were low and narrow, brought further to Paul's Wharf in barges, and finally dragged up to the Cathedral. Arrangements for supervision, both in Dorset and in London, were to be a constant source of trouble. And on one occasion when England was at war with France, a ship carrying stone was captured, taken to Calais,

92 St Paul's Cathedral. Design for the south side

and sold to a merchant of Rotterdam, and had to be bought back. Portland stone was used for all exterior work, but the accounts show that Reigate, Headington and Ketton stone was supplied for part of the interior.

The staff, too, was changing and increasing. Edward Woodroffe died in October 1675, and was replaced in the next year by John Oliver, one of the Surveyors appointed by the City on the Commission for rebuilding the City churches. He was to remain as Deputy-Surveyor till 1701. Joshua Marshall died in 1678, and was succeeded as both Master Mason to the Crown and one of the contractors for St Paul's by Thomas Wise. At about the same time, the volume of work had so far grown that it became necessary to spread the load, and two more contractors, Edward Pierce and Jasper Latham, appear in the books. As with the original contractors, all were known to Wren for their work on the City churches. And in 1681, Thomas Strong, who had built St Stephen, Walbrook and worked on St Paul's since the laying of the foundation-stone, was replaced by his younger brother Edward, who was to work on the building for more than twenty-five years.

Progress year by year of the vast undertaking can be followed in detail in the accounts. The four mason-contractors were allotted sections of the building, in which they were responsible for the laying and carving of stone and sometimes for making models of details: but the host of other workers sent in separate accounts. There were carpenters who were endlessly setting up and moving scaffolding, bricklayers who worked the vaults before they were plastered, plumbers who provided lead for the roofs, and labourers who had a variety of tasks from covering the half-finished walls with rubble to save them from frost, carrying molten lead to the masons for setting cramps in the stone-work, or washing the newly carved work with lime water. The accounts were signed quarterly by both Wren and John Oliver, and Wren is known to have visited the works every Saturday.

The accounts and the Contract Book make it evident that quite early in the operations Wren had decided to ignore the terms of the Warrant which directed him to build and finish 'by parts'. It had clearly implied that the choir only was first to be built and completed and put into use. But as early as March 1676 Marshall and Strong signed contracts for the south-west and north-west 'Peer or Legg of the Dome', and in 1678 Pierce was directed to work on the exterior of the south transept. Work, indeed, was moving in many directions at the same time and it is likely that Wren, having got his team of skilled men together, was determined to proceed with the whole building. Had he finished the choir, interest might slacken, the flow of money might cease, and men might move to other jobs and it would be hard to collect them again.

By 1684 Edward Strong was working on the north side of the nave, in the next year Edward Pierce contracted to set and carve the great cornice inside the choir. In 1687 the coal tax, first imposed twenty years earlier, was extended and since the City churches were now almost finished, the larger part of the money was in future to be devoted to St Paul's. Two new master masons, Samuel Fulkes and Christopher Kempster, were added to the team, and Fulkes began to work on the west end in August 1688.

By now, further important modifications had been made to the Warrant plan, for the nave had been reduced from five bays to three, thereby balancing the three bays of the choir and increasing the idea, so perfectly expressed in the Great Model, of a centrally-planned church. At the west end of the nave one larger bay, to be covered by a small dome, was added, while on each side of it were chapels. It is said that these chapels, begun in 1687, were the direct wish of King James II, who was hoping soon to restore Roman Catholicism in England. In fact, since they were hardly begun by the time of James's flight in 1688, only that one on the south was fitted as a chapel, being called the Morning Prayer Chapel, while the one on the north was used as the Consistory Court. Today they are the Chapels of St Dunstan and St Michael and St George. Wren must have welcomed the chapels, for on the exterior their projection helped to break the effect of length of the nave, and in the interior they, with the larger bay, gave an opportunity for varying the space composition.

The effect of the alteration in the coal tax is quickly seen in the accounts, nearly £34,000 being spent in 1687–88, as against £12,346 in the previous year. In later years the amount varied considerably, but when the final accounts were made up in 1710 it was shown that £738,845 5s. 2½d. had been spent on the Cathedral, a vast sum for the times, and the equal of many millions in modern money.

By October 1694 the masonry of the choir was at last finished, inside and out, but there were not yet any fittings and much remained to be done further westward. Contracts were signed with Bernard Smith for the organ and with Jean Tijou, a Huguenot refugee, for the iron gates for the choir, and work began on the choir-stalls. Considerable delay in proceeding with the rest of the church was caused by a serious landslide at the Portland quarries in 1696; the leading masons were sent down to inspect the damage, and Wren himself went in May 1697 with Edward Strong and Nicholas Hawksmoor, who was now Wren's leading draughtsman. Two months earlier, Parliament had grown restive at the slow progress of the work, and had adopted the mean expedient of suspending half Wren's salary until the Cathedral was finished. At last, on 2 December 1697, the choir was opened for the Thanksgiving Service for the Peace of Ryswick, and on the 5th the first Sunday service was held in the new Cathedral. It was, however, to be about another ten years before the whole work was done. The west towers were built by Fulkes and Kempster between 1705 and 1708, the clock for the south-west tower being ordered at the end of 1706, and the west end being roofed at about the same time. Lastly, the design of the dome, which had been a major consideration ever since Marshall and Strong had begun the legs in 1676, seems to have been finalized in about 1705–06, but was still to take some years to build. A model was made of it in December 1706, and after a disagreeable controversy with vested interests, who tried to push copper against Wren's will as the covering for the dome, tarred cloths were put up in April 1708 'to cover the workmen in hot and wet weather upon the Leading ye Roofe of the Dome'. Leading was still going on a year later. On 29 June 1708 Wren made a careful measured drawing for the cross and the ball which surmounted the lantern. It shows the cross to be 12 feet 6 inches high, and is perhaps the last of Wren's drawings which has survived. The coppersmith was paid for carrying out the design in October of the same year, but strangely enough there is no entry in the accounts for its erection. Nor can it be said with certainty precisely when the building was finished. Wren's son declares in *Parentalia* that he himself, deputed by his father, laid the last stone in 1710: and at the end of 1711 Parliament declared the work was complete and the arrears of Wren's salary were paid. It was thirty-six years since the laying of the foundation-stone in 1675. Few, if any, comparable buildings were achieved by a single architect within his own lifetime.

The building history has, for convenience, been sketched *Ill. 89* first, and it is now necessary to go back in time and examine the fabric in detail. It has already been shown that almost immediately after the issue of the Warrant in May 1675, basic alterations were made to the design then accepted. For the two-storeyed elevation of the walls, Wren turned to the one great classical building in London, Inigo Jones's Banqueting House. From it he took the motive of pilasters set in front of a channelled wall, and since the scale of his building was so much larger he used the coupled pilasters at the ends of Jones's façade, for they give a stronger accent, and single pilasters might have looked a little mean. From Jones too he took the relatively rare device of carved festoons at the level of the capitals. Jones's pilasters are Ionic below and Corinthian above. Wren, whose interest in a rich surface texture is one of the most striking features of the exterior of the Cathedral, uses Corinthian below and Composite above, the capitals of both orders therefore making strong patches of carving at the top of each pair of pilasters. It is possible that the use of a basement, with small windows lighting the crypt, which did not appear in the Warrant design, is also taken from the Banqueting House.

The window treatment, however, owes nothing to Jones. The round-headed windows in the lower storey, which light the aisles, have a fairly shallow moulded surround with lugged architraves where the curve turns to the vertical below, and are somewhat French in character. In the upper storey, which is the screen wall, the features look at first glance like windows but are in fact niches. Each is set in a little tabernacle, composed of two small Corinthian columns carrying a pediment, a motive almost certainly borrowed by Wren from Serlio's reconstruction of the Pantheon. The small windows below each niche are not false windows, but have a vital role, for they light the

94 St Paul's Cathedral. Grinling Gibbons' sculpture below window on south transept

passages, invisible from both inside and out, which run the *Ill. 88* whole length of the Cathedral above the aisle vaults, and beneath the sloping lead roofs which cover them.

It is only since the recent cleaning of the stone-work that it has become possible to appreciate the extraordinary richness of the surface decoration, which hardly recurs in any other of Wren's works. The forms used are small, fruit, flowers and foliage, and *Ill. 93* though they are in fairly high relief, the effects of light and shade are not strong enough to break into the solidity of the wall. This particular use of over-all decoration can hardly have been developed from Italian engraved sources, and it is more likely that Wren was drawing on his recollection of sixteenth- or very early seventeenth-century buildings he had seen in Paris. The Great Court of the Louvre, the Hôtel de Sully, and even the façade of Saint Paul-Saint Louis, all have much rich decoration, though in France the human figure generally forms part of it.

The decorative carving on St Paul's was mainly, as has been said, carried out by the mason-contractor responsible for the various sections of the work. Most of it dates from the late 1680s and the early 1690s, but it must have been planned very early, so that allowance for it could be made in the shaping of the stone. A little of the work, however, was done by sculptors. The wonderfully inventive carved panels below the great *Ill. 94* round-headed windows are the work of Grinling Gibbons, who

93 St Paul's Cathedral. West front, sculpture above window at base of north tower

95 St Paul's Cathedral. South transept pediment with the phoenix carved by Caius Gabriel Cibber

was paid for them in September 1694 and May 1695. There are twenty-six of them, no two being identical. The similar panels on the west chapels are by the carver, Jonathan Maine, who also did fine work inside the Cathedral.

The transept fronts are even more richly decorated, for ropes of fruit and flowers hang down beside the central windows, and both the pediments above have carving set in curved lunettes. *Ill. 95* That on the south transept, by Caius Gabriel Cibber, shows a phoenix rising from the ashes, thus taking up the theme of *Resurgam*. The north pediment, cut by Gibbons, is much less striking in design, and contains the Royal Arms flanked by two somewhat awkward angels. The most beautiful features of the *Ill. 96* transept fronts, however, are the two semicircular porticoes which have replaced the flat colonnades of the Warrant design.

These are almost certainly an adaptation of the façade of Santa
Maria della Pace in Rome, and the pediment with a lunette in
it may have come from the same source – Hooke had bought an
engraving of the Italian building in 1677, and Wren probably
by now knew Falda's *Chiese di Roma*. Wren's portico is less
complex than that of Pietro da Cortona, but it is beautifully
designed, and in its semicircle prepares the eye for the great
circle of the dome above.

    The transepts make the first break in the uniform design of the
exterior; the second occurs on the north and south fronts of the
west chapels. First the design of the lower storey is modified by
the introduction of niches, and then the final window intro-
duces a new motive. It is set back in the thickness of the wall, the   *Ill. 93*
sense of depth being strengthened by the use of false perspective

96 St Paul's Cathedral.
South transept front

in its surrounds, a device taken from Borromini. These windows are repeated on the west front, at the base of the towers.

Ill. 97   The west front is, perhaps, the least impressive part of the exterior of St Paul's, but it can be seen as a typical Wren compromise. Several drawings exist showing a single-order portico

Ill. 98   of giant columns. One of these, drawn by Nicholas Hawksmoor, bears an inscription referring to King William and Queen Mary, and so can be dated between 1688 and the Queen's death in 1694. There can be no doubt that such a portico would have given a greater grandeur to the building. But according to *Parentalia*, Wren was prevented from building his giant portico because the Portland quarries could not produce blocks of stone long enough to span the intercolumniations of the entablature. This had been possible for Jones's famous portico; but Jones's columns were 50 feet high and Wren's would have been 90 feet

97 St Paul's Cathedral. West front

98 St Paul's Cathedral. Drawing for giant order at west end

and the intercolumniations much greater. Wren was therefore forced back to a two-storey design, which retains the proportions of the main elevation. But, since single columns might well have looked a little meagre, he couples his columns, thereby achieving stronger accents of light and shadow. The pediment above contains a relief, not perhaps sufficiently appreciated, of the Conversion of St Paul, by the sculptor Francis Bird, one of the most successful examples of Baroque sculpture in England.

If the west front is slightly pedestrian, the same cannot be said of the last features of the exterior – the west towers and the dome, for they are perhaps the summit of Wren's achievement. *Ills. 101,* Neither design was fixed until after the turn of the century, for *102* between 1701 and 1703 a set of official engravings of the building was published. These still show the west towers closely based on the design of Bramante's Tempietto, while the dome is on

Ill. 21 the Michelangelo model. One drawing for the west towers, partly if not wholly in Wren's own hand, is dated: 'Feb. 25th, 1703/4'; work on them extended from about 1705 to 1708. The north-west tower was built by Samuel Fulkes and the south-west by William Kempster. The latter contains a remarkable *Ill. 99* circular staircase leading up to the library above the chapel of St Michael and St George, while at its foot, on the south side, is *Ill. 100* the beautiful Dean's door, with scrolls, wreaths and cherubs' heads as fine as anything cut by Gibbons. It is good to read that when Kempster was paid in June 1705, he was given an additional £20 for 'Extraordinary Diligence and Care used in the said carving and his good performance of the same.' It is not surprising that Wren's labour problems were small and that he kept his men, for it is clear that he appreciated and encouraged good work.

99 St Paul's Cathedral. Circular stair in south-west tower

100 St Paul's Cathedral. Upper part of Dean's door carved by William Kempster

The west towers belong to that late group of steeples with *Ill. 101* columns standing out from a central core, though here the design is extremely complex. A ring of columns is arranged round the inner circular core, two visible above each face of the square tower below, while between them two further paired columns stand out over the angles of the tower. Above this storey, full of contrasts of light and shadow, the tower diminishes upwards to an ogee cap crowned by a gilt copper pineapple, the changes from one storey to the next being softened by the use of vases or brackets, carrying the eye easily upwards. It is possible that the basic design of paired columns standing out from a curved core is borrowed from Francesco Borromini's

101 St Paul's Cathedral. South-west tower

102 St Paul's Cathedral from the south

façade of S. Agnese in the Piazza Navona in Rome; and it certainly seems that here, in the window already described at the base of the towers, and in the steeple of St Vedast, Foster Lane, a few years earlier, Wren displays an interest in Borromini's work. The proportions, and above all the effects of light and shade are, however, totally different. Wren's design is less sophisticated but, surprisingly, more massive in its members and with stronger contrasts of light and shade. In their variety of outline, which changes as the eye moves round the building, the west towers were surely designed as a foil to the grand simplicity of the dome.

Ill. 102 Many drawings exist for the dome, but none is dated, so it is not possible to follow the steps by which the final design was evolved about 1704. Wren must have thought for many years on the problems of dome design, and though his final solution contains ideas from other architects, it is in no sense a pastiche, but has many new and highly original features. The great

103 St Paul's Cathedral. Detail of drum of dome

circular drum from which the dome rises is surrounded by a ring of columns, evenly spaced, and carrying an entablature and a balustrade which swings in an unbroken ring round the dome. This drum, with its simplicity, which presents a striking contrast to the broken outlines of the west towers, comes of course from Bramante. But something of vital importance has been added. Every fourth intercolumniation is not open, but solid, *Ill. 103* though to prevent the contrast from being too great, a niche has *Ill. 104* been set on the face, with a panel of ornament above. This variation in the rhythm is not inserted only, or even chiefly, for visual purposes, for the solid portions are indeed buttresses which help to control the thrust of the dome. It is almost as if Wren had added Michelangelo's paired columns within the ring of Bramante's drum.

Above the drum is a kind of attic decorated with pilasters and with square windows framed by simple mouldings. Then the lead-covered dome, with vertical ribs on its surface, soars up

104 St Paul's
Cathedral. Detail
of niche in
drum of dome

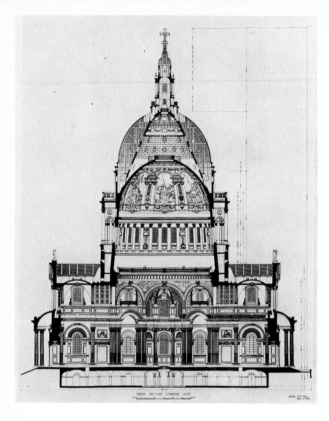

to the large stone lantern, in which there is an echo of the paired
columns of the west towers, but in a quieter key, for the
entablatures are straight and not curved. Last comes the ball and
the cross.

In the dome, Wren achieved a work of great beauty and
serenity. This is immediately clear to the eye, but what is hidden
below the lead covering reveals that it is also a piece of brilliant
construction in which Wren faced and overcame a variety of
problems. To understand this the dome must be considered
from the inside as well as the outside, and even then there are
vital parts of the structure which are hidden from sight.

From his first association with St Paul's before the Great Fire,
he was anxious that the dome should be high, providing a land-
mark comparable to the tower of the old Cathedral. This he

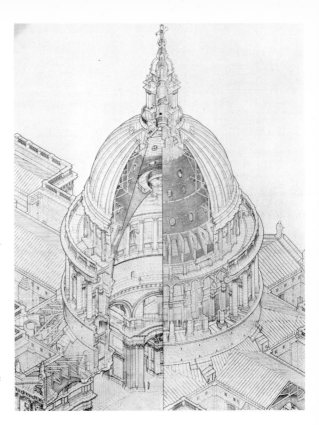

106 St Paul's Cathedral.
Isometric section of dome

achieves by constructing a dome which is ovoid and not semi-   *Ill. 105*
circular, set on an unusually high attic above the large drum.
The structure is further heightened by the large stone lantern,
and the cross at the top which is 365 feet above ground level. The
effect of such a tall dome, when standing inside it, would, however, have been extremely disagreeable, for it would have
seemed like a tall chimney or funnel over the middle of the
church. Wren therefore constructed a low semicircular dome,
with a round hole (or eye) in the middle. This dome is high
enough to be impressive from the inside, but is at the same time
a comfortable covering for the great central space. It is lit by
windows behind the open colonnades of the drum, but light
also streams down through the central eye. This is less easy to
understand, and is indeed the only indication that something is

hidden, and not visible from either outside or inside. Two layers, the inner and the outer dome have been described, but the section reveals that there is in fact a third layer. This is a tall cone of brick, set between the inner and the outer dome. It is this which carries the weight of the lantern, which could not possibly be borne by the outer dome, constructed of timber covered with lead. At the top of the cone are openings through which light falls from windows just below the lantern and invisible from the ground outside, though they can be seen by looking up through the eye of the inner dome. The weight, and consequently the thrust, of the whole construction is enormous. Among the devices used to control it are iron girdles or chains set in the stone-work, the largest, just above the top of the drum, being the work of Jean Tijou. These chains, and indeed the whole handling of the cone and the stone-work of the drum, which can be well seen in the isometric section, help to drive the thrust downwards, partly on to the main piers, but partly on to the outer walls, where it is further contained by the screen walls pressing against the transepts.

Ill. 106

Ill. 91

Ill. 107
    A long time is needed for appreciating the outside of the Cathedral, so rich in detail. The interior is perhaps more quickly grasped, though it, too, has beauties of detail which are worth careful study. The first impression on entering from the west doors is of a building radiant with light. In the restoration necessary after the Second World War, the Victorian glass was removed, and Wren's simple harmony of creamy-grey and brownish stone, with adornment at certain points by gilding, can now be enjoyed to the full. Some Victorian decoration remains in the mosaic decoration in the roof of the choir and above the main arches under the dome, but it tones well enough with the rest of the interior.

    It has already been noted that Wren, in discarding the Warrant plan, made both nave and choir of three bays with a larger bay to the west. The piers defining the bays are solid, as they must be for weight-carrying, but they do not appear heavy, for the main face has a tall Corinthian pilaster, with a

107 St Paul's Cathedral. Interior looking east

full entablature very richly carved, running the length of the church. The side faces have a pair of shorter Corinthian pilasters, unfluted, which act as imposts for the arches dividing the centre from the side aisles. These arches are decorated with coffering, which is also to be seen under the great arches of the dome. It may well be that Wren had retained a memory of perhaps the most beautiful church he had seen in Paris, the *Ill. 19* Val-de-Grâce, for the main design of the piers is not dissimilar, though altered to suit the far larger scale, and coffering is also a feature of the church.

Over the main entablature is a fine ironwork balcony, gilded, and above this rise the arches across the church, dividing bay from bay. These are of darker stone, probably Ketton – the piers are Portland stone – and their soffits are decorated by a rich intertwining guilloche. In the Warrant plan, bays of both nave and choir were to be covered by cross-vaults, but in execution all are covered with saucer domes. These have both a con-structional and an aesthetic advantage. They are built of brick, plastered over, and so are lighter than stone vaults and have less thrust; and their circular pattern, emphasized by the ring of brown stone from which they rise, announces the great circle in the centre of the church.

In both the Warrant and the final plan (and in the Great Model also), the dome is set on eight piers, carrying eight great arches. In the Warrant plan the aisles are half the width of the nave, so that one aisle of the nave, coming to the central area,

108 St Paul's Cathedral. Central space looking north-west

109 St Paul's Cathedral.
Central space looking
north-east as originally
planned

joins with one aisle of the transept, and produces a space to be
spanned which is the exact equal of the space next to it, that is,
of the centre aisle of the nave. The eight arches carried by such
evenly spaced piers would, automatically, be equal in height.
But in his change from the Warrant, Wren had reduced the
width of the side aisles when increasing the thickness of the
outer walls, so that when he got to the dome area he found
himself with unequal intervals between the piers, for those produced by the side and transept aisles are smaller. The eight
arches carried by the piers would not, therefore, automatically
rise to the same height. Wren's solution cannot have been an *Ill. 108*
easy one. Over the wide spaces of choir, nave and transepts are
great semicircular arches, with three rows of coffering. Between
them are lower, elliptical arches, spanning the narrower aisles,
and only rising to about the level of the springing of the great
arches. But, so that the impression of eight great arches will be
received, a second arch, to the same height as the great arch, is
thrown across the narrower space. The junction of the two is a
little uncomfortable for the inserted arch does not spring
happily from the pier below it. Like the design of the west front,
it must be accepted as a compromise. On the other hand, Wren
makes good use of the space left between the lower arch and the
inserted arch, for as at St Stephen, Walbrook, though by

125

different means and on a far greater scale, he inserts portions of vaulting to carry some of the thrust on to the outer walls.

The great central space which Wren had so much desired, and had achieved, makes even now an overwhelming impact. Could it be seen as he left it, the effect would be even greater. For he closed the space on the east side by setting a screen across the choir, with the great organ above it, thus stressing the centralized planning of the church. There was a practical as well as an aesthetic reason for this. The choir was amply large enough for the daily services, and for a State occasion, seats could be erected in the great empty space under the dome. Unfortunately, the mid-Victorians, who disapproved of St Paul's because it was not Gothic, and so to their minds un-English, did much to destroy Wren's interior design. The screen and organ were taken down in 1860, in 1870 the organ was rebuilt in two parts on either side of the choir, and columns from the screen were moved to the end of the transepts, some being destroyed in the Second World War. The floor of the choir was raised, the arrangement of the choir-stalls altered, and much dark stained glass, fortunately now removed, was inserted in the windows. In 1888 a monstrous pink marble reredos was erected, closing the vista through nave and choir with an unfortunate anticlimax.

Luckily this no longer exists. One of the two high-explosive bombs which hit the building in 1940–41 caused the destruction of both altar and reredos. The latter has not been replaced. Instead the new altar is covered by a baldacchino of wood, based on a model left by Wren. With its twisted columns and great tasselled canopy it echoes on a less majestic scale Bernini's bronze masterpiece in St Peter's, and is a fitting culmination to the church.

The fittings are of superb quality, and mercifully survived the war with little damage. The choir-stalls, and the carved screens behind them facing the aisles, are the work of Grinling Gibbons, and show him at his best. His endlessly fertile invention and his great technical skill appear in the combination of

Ill. 109

Ills. 107, 114

Ill. 110

126

110 St Paul's Cathedral. Choir-stalls by Grinling Gibbons

cherubs' heads set between scrolls, which break forward and give a three-dimensional quality to the frieze they adorn, while below them is a riot of fruit and flowers, with carved panels each different from the next. The Bishop's throne and the Lord *Ill. 112* Mayor's seat are marked by canopies in which heads, scrolls and flowers are treated in the round. No less fine, but rightly more subdued, are the backs of the stalls to the aisles. It would seem *Ill. 111* that Wren gave Gibbons a fairly free hand, for drawings for the backs remain in which the architectural features are set out by one of Wren's draughtsmen, and the design of the carving sketched in the rapid pen strokes of Gibbons. He was also responsible for the elaborate organ case, which is adorned by angels as well as the usual fruit and flowers. The rich carving in stone on the spandrels behind the lesser arches of the dome is his, but fails to be impressive owing to over-intricacy, the wealth of flowers being on too small a scale. Gibbons was, indeed, at his

127

111 St Paul's Cathedral. Screen at rear of choir-stalls

112 St Paul's Cathedral. Bishop's throne by Grinling Gibbons

113 St Paul's Cathedral. Chapel of St Michael and St George with screen by Jonathan Maine

best as a wood-carver, and the bolder and somewhat coarser detailing by masons, such as the shields in the wreaths of the nave cupolas, by Edward Strong and Thomas Wise, fulfil their purpose better than Gibbons' tulips and primroses. He was, however, not the only wood-carver to produce work of distinction, for the fine screens of the western chapels are the work of Jonathan Maine.

Ill. 113

In addition to much carved ornament in stone and wood, St Paul's has magnificent ironwork. Wren was lucky in being

able to employ the highly skilled Huguenot, Jean Tijou. The
Ill. 114 superb wrought-iron gates, rich with acanthus decoration, near
the east end of the choir are his, as are the somewhat less spec-
tacular grilles in the outer side of the choir-stalls. The choir
gates have recently been cleaned and regilded, and with the new
baldacchino, which also has much gilding, give a fair idea of the
richness of decoration Wren thought fitting for the sanctuary
of the Cathedral.

Wren's long and brilliant control of the operations at St
Paul's ended sadly. In 1711 he petitioned for the full payment
of his salary, and notes somewhat bitterly that the remaining
work had been taken out of his hands. A mean intrigue had
defeated his wish to surround the Cathedral with a railing of
wrought iron, and an iron-founder of dubious character was
commissioned to make it in cast iron. Further evidence of
intrigue appears in the decision to finish the top of the walls with
a balustrade. The old man, now about eighty-four, reacted
strongly against this, both on sound architectural grounds, and
on the foolishness of modern taste: 'Persons with little skill in
architecture did expect, I believe, to see something they had
been used to in Gothic structures: *and ladies think nothing well
without an edging*'. Wren's last attendance at a meeting of the
Commission took place in July 1715, by which time, against
his wishes, Thornhill's designs for the painting of the cupola had
been accepted. Although still technically Surveyor to the
Cathedral, he thereafter left the supervision in the hands of the
Assistant-Surveyor, John James.

The quality of St Paul's, with its triumphs and its compromises, can be understood only if all the limiting conditions
are remembered. Wren was building, in the age of the Late
Baroque, for a Protestant community, and a conservative
clergy, who wished to preserve the Latin cross plan which they
had inherited from the Middle Ages. Money was short, materials came in slowly and, at the beginning of the work at least,
Wren lacked experience as an architect. He gained it by ceaselessly adapting himself to circumstances and using his mathe-

114 St Paul's Cathedral. Wrought-iron gates on
north side of choir by Jean Tijou

matical genius to overcome difficulties. The reputation of St Paul's has varied greatly in the 250 years since it was built. In the eighteenth century, the triumph of Palladianism was so great that Wren was held to have 'ability but no taste'. The nineteenth century, as has been said, frankly disliked the building. In the early years of this century it was fairly firmly held that Wren was a great man, and St Paul's a fine example of 'Late Renaissance' style. More recently, with the interest in and understanding of Continental Baroque, St Paul's has been regarded as a little tame – in fact, as a Baroque building which fails. This view ignores the circumstances under which the Cathedral was commissioned, and the needs of the society for which it was built. Wren's triumph lies in his conquest of circumstances; and surely by any standards the design for the dome is great architecture. His own generation had no doubt about his quality. To them, the man had matched the moment. In 1696–97 John Evelyn, in his rededication to Wren of his translation (first published in 1664) of Fréart's *Parallels* wrote: 'I have named St Paul's, and truly not without admiration, as oft as I recall to mind (as frequently I do) the deplorable condition it was in when (after it had been made a stable for horses, and a den of thieves) You (with other gentlemen and myself) were by the late King Charles named Commissioners to survey the dilapidations, and to make a report to His Majesty, in order to a speedy reparation. . . . You will not forget the struggle we had with some, who were for patching it up anyhow. . . . When (to put an end to the contest) five days after that Dreadful Conflagration happened, out of whose ashes this Phoenix is risen, and was by Providence designed for you: the circumstance is too remarkable, that I could not pass it over without notice.'

In the last twenty years, St Paul's has again been transformed. The blackened building no longer stands on the top of Ludgate Hill, but instead a masterpiece in pale golden stone, with an enriched surface which was impossible to appreciate in its former state. It is almost as if Evelyn's Phoenix had risen again.

CHAPTER SIX

Secular buildings before 1688

The planning and building of St Paul's, and to a lesser extent the work on the City churches, must have occupied Wren's mind continuously from about 1668 to his retirement in 1718. Nevertheless, he also found time for a number of secular buildings, some of considerable size. Most of them were commissioned by the Crown, and were therefore part of his duties as Surveyor-General; but a few were for other patrons.

About 1674 the University of Cambridge considered the question of building a Senate House in emulation of the recently completed Sheldonian Theatre at Oxford. As at Oxford, University ceremonies took place in the University Church, and it was felt by some that this was unsuitable. One of the chief advocates of the new idea was Dr Isaac Barrow, Master of Trinity College, a mathematician well known to Wren. Support appears to have been half-hearted, and the scheme was soon abandoned for lack of funds. By that time, however, Wren had produced a design for a large but ungainly building which included a great hall of basilican type together with a large library. The basilican hall comes from Palladio, but *Ill. 115* much of the detail is taken from Serlio. Probably, if the design had gone forward, Wren would have adjusted it in execution, as he did on so many other occasions, but judging it from the remaining drawings, it was no great loss.

Dr Barrow, however, was exceedingly angry with the University for its apathy, and determined to show what a single college could do. According to tradition, he went back to Trinity College after the discussion and 'that very afternoon he, with his gardeners and servants, staked out the very foundation upon which the building now stands'. Unfortunately, it is difficult to reconcile this endearing picture of an angry academic

115 Senate House, Cambridge. Elevation

with what can be deduced from the drawings for Trinity College Library, but at least the circumstances led to the creation of one of Wren's finest buildings.

The new Library was to stand at the west end of Nevile's Court, an extension to the College built in the early seventeenth century, consisting of two arcaded blocks containing lodgings, *Ills. 116,* running from the Hall towards the river. Wren's first design, *117* which is undated, was for an isolated building, square without and circular within, joined to the ends of the earlier blocks by a low curved wall and iron railings. Since it was to be covered by a dome, and has an applied portico of Ionic columns, there can be little doubt that the design was borrowed from Palladio's *Ill. 118* Villa Rotonda. The plate in Palladio's *I Quattro Libri* shows a dome similar to Wren's, and not the low dome now on the Villa, which was executed by Scamozzi. The drawings for this abortive design are interesting, for they show that Wren had already considered the needs of a library, and had arranged bookstacks well lit from above, and tables below them for readers.

134

116, 117 Trinity College Library, Cambridge. First scheme, plan and elevation

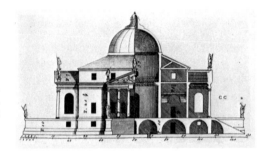

118 Andrea Palladio.
Villa Rotonda, Vicenza.
Elevation and section

It is not known why or when this design was abandoned, but
in February 1676 work was begun on the existing Library. This
is a long two-storeyed block set right across the end of Nevile's *Ill. 119*
Court, with its back looking on to the river. We have fuller
information about Wren's ideas concerning the design of this
building than for any other of his works, for when he sent a
number of drawings to Dr Barrow, he also sent a long letter
explaining his reasons for various features. Both the letter and
the drawings are now at All Souls College, Oxford. The front
towards the Court is open on the lower storey (like the earlier

Ill. 121 side blocks); at the back the same storey is closed, while between
Ill. 120 the back wall and the front arcade is a row of columns which
help to support the floor of the Library above. Wren's explana-
tion of this arrangement is that it is 'according to the manner of
the ancients, who made double walks (with three rows of
pillars, or two rows and a wall) about the forum'. This direct
reference to the authority of antiquity is revealing and shows
how carefully Wren studied such information as was available
to him. In this case, his knowledge of a Roman forum is certainly based on the plate in Palladio's book.

Wren's arguments cannot here be followed in detail, interesting though they are. His chief problem was to marry the new
design to the old Court, and to arrange access from the first
floor of the side wings into the Library. In fact this last requirement was abandoned, but not until the Library was built.

Ill. 119 In the building as executed the Doric order of the lower
storey is higher than the side loggias, but the openings are not,

119 Trinity College Library, Cambridge, Nevile's Court

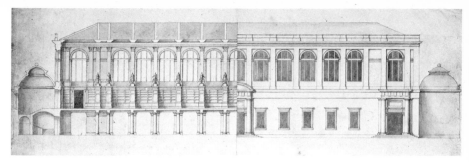

120 Trinity College Library, Cambridge. Design for longitudinal section and elevation towards river

for they do not rise to the height of the arches between the columns. The heads of these arches are filled with carved lunettes, so that the openings between the columns are square-headed, but equal in height to the side loggias. In case Dr Barrow thought the solid lunettes unorthodox, Wren explained that he had 'seen the effect abroad in good buildings', meaning perhaps the Collège de France by Louis Le Vau. The

121 Trinity College Library, Cambridge, river front

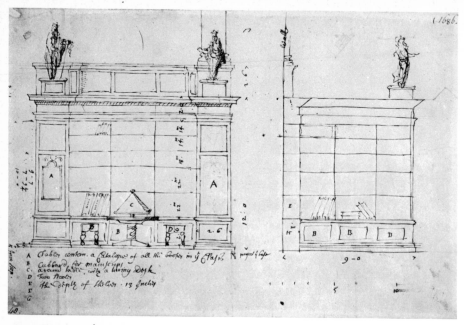

122 Trinity College Library, Cambridge. Sketch for bookcase and desk

124 Trinity College Library, Cambridge

123 Trinity College Library, Cambridge. Alcove showing desk

Doric order carries a full entablature, the cornice making a strong horizontal, while above it, the upper storey has an Ionic order, also with arched openings between, though these are glazed and are thus very large windows. In appearance, therefore, the design with its superimposed orders, with round-headed openings between, is very similar to Wren's design for the First Model for St Paul's. Both, perhaps, go back to a famous building of antiquity, the Theatre of Marcellus in Rome. *Ill. 76*

The design, however, is not quite so straightforward as it looks. The firm horizontal between the lower order and the windows above, leads one to suppose that it represents the division of the interior, and that the floor of the Library corresponds with the line of the Doric cornice. This is not the case, for the floor is dropped to the springing of the lower arches. It was chiefly for this reason that Wren filled in the lunettes. The great advantage of this device is that the book-stacks could be set below the windows, and readers would *Ill. 124* enjoy an excellent light from above.

Wren took immense trouble over the arrangement of the interior. He designed bookstacks both along and at right angles to the walls, so that students should have a square table and two chairs in each cell, drawings of this furniture being provided.

Tables, book rests and stools of Wren's design may still be seen in the Library. He also advised marble paving for the 'middle alley', because footsteps would not make so much noise on it, though the cells between the bookcases should be floored in wood which would make less dust.

The set of drawings which accompanied the letter are extremely fine and certainly by Wren himself; but because he was working with a mason he did not know, Robert Grumbold, he ended his letter saying: 'I suppose you have good masons, however, I would willingly take a further paines to give all the mouldings in great, we are scrupulous in small matters, the Architects are as great pedants as Critics or Heralds.' One drawing showing details of mouldings has survived, though detached from the rest. It is hardly a full-size detail as understood today, but all the measurements are given and a good mason, as Grumbold proved to be, could certainly have worked from it.

The finishing of the Library was slow. The fabric and the main interior fittings were finished about 1688, but it was not until after 1690 that the final decoration was completed by Grinling Gibbons. He supplied busts to stand on the bookcases (instead of the statues shown in Wren's drawing), as well as much fine carving. The building, both inside and out, remains much as Wren left it, and in its firm clarity of design, combined now with a mastery of detail far greater than in his earlier Cambridge works, it can be ranked with the finest of his creations. In its bold use of orders and its careful balance between horizontals and verticals, it is the most Italian of his works, and

provides an interesting contrast to Hooke's Bedlam Hospital begun in the same year, which shows the broken roof-line characteristic of Northern architecture.

Wren's personal links with academic circles made it inevitable that he should be consulted on several occasions, sometimes

125 Tom Tower, Christ Church, Oxford

probably about designs which were not his own. But in 1681 he was asked by the Dean of Christ Church, Oxford, to complete the main entrance to Cardinal Wolsey's Great Quadrangle, always known as Tom Tower. The two lower storeys with their flanking turrets are mainly of early sixteenth-century design, and Wren's first letter about the completion of the tower states: 'I resolved it ought to be Gothick to agree with the Founder's Worke, Yet I have not continued soe busy as he began.' Once again, as in his report of Salisbury Cathedral, Wren shows a respect for Gothic architecture, and though his upper part of Tom Tower has not the richly fretted surface of the Late Perpendicular work below, there is no abrupt break in style, and the new work completes the composition with dignity.

Ill. 125

Three other projects of the 1670s must be mentioned here, two of which were executed and the other abandoned. The great Doric column, carrying a flaming urn, near the north end *Ill. 126* of London Bridge, and known simply as the Monument, was erected by Parliament in commemoration of the Great Fire. Dr Robert Hooke was associated with Wren in the work, which was finished in 1676, and it is impossible to be certain of the part played by the two architects. A number of alternative designs exist, none in Wren's own hand, but it is known that he disliked the urn, and would have preferred a statue of the King or a great copper ball surrounded by flames.

Ill. 127   The project for a mausoleum for Charles I, to be set up at Windsor, dates from 1678 and is, architecturally, far more interesting and distinguished. Like Trinity College Library, so

126 The Monument, London

127 Mausoleum for
Charles I

near to it in date, it is purely Italian in inspiration. The design
shows a circular domed building, some 70 feet in diameter,
with the interior arranged as a quatrefoil, with four great
niches. The main idea, which must surely be taken from
Bramante's Tempietto, is a cylinder within a cylinder. The
lower, larger cylinder is not open as in the Tempietto, but has
evenly spaced Corinthian half-columns set in front of a
channelled wall, in this and in the frieze of festoons at the level
of the capitals, suggesting a slightly more plastic version of
Inigo Jones's Banqueting House. The entablature carries a
parapet, which was to support twenty standing figures, these
serving to soften the change to the smaller cylinder. This consisted of a high base, broken by niches and windows, while

143

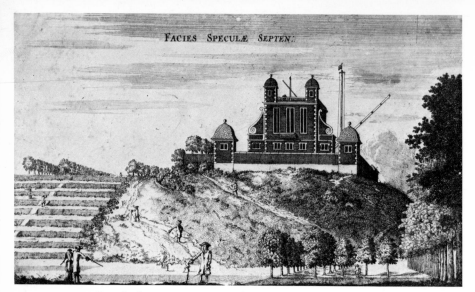

128 Royal Observatory, Greenwich

above it was a small version of Michelangelo's dome of St Peter's, with its buttresses round the drum and its ribs running up to a lantern. The whole was to be topped by a figure of Fame, with trumpet and wreath. Within was to stand an elaborate sculptured group of the Royal Martyr, supported by Virtues trampling on Vices. Although in January 1678 Parliament voted the sum of £70,000 'for a solemn funeral for his late Majesty King Charles the First and to erect a Monument for the said Prince of glorious memory', the money was presumably never paid, and nothing came of the project.

Ill. 128   The third commission, the Royal Observatory at Greenwich, must have been of special interest to Wren, in view of his own former association with astronomy. It was built by order of the King in 1675 for the use of John Flamsteed, the first Astronomer Royal, who had been appointed in that year. Flamsteed's contribution to knowledge was considerable, for he made the first trustworthy catalogue of the fixed stars, and Newton was to build on his lunar observations. Later in life, when he was

144

having difficulties about the publication of his works, he recorded a striking tribute to Wren's character, writing: 'He is a very sincere honest man: I find him so, and perhaps the only honest person I have to deal with.'

The Observatory, set on a hill on the site of a former castle, was largely built of old material, and is completely un-Italian in design. On each side of a central building, which contains one great octagonal room on the first floor, are turrets with domical roofs in the Jacobean manner, and the joining of the centre to the side blocks is masked by large scrolls. It seems almost certain that Wren was consciously attempting a slightly fantastic, castle-like building, for when in 1681 he was building Tom Tower, he wrote to Bishop Fell, who was considering the possibility of using the Tower as an observatory: 'Wee built indeed an Observatory at Greenwich not unlike what your Tower will prove, it was for the Observator's habitation and a little for Pompe.'

Up to 1680 all Wren's buildings, with the exception of his relatively modest work at Emmanuel College, Cambridge, had been single-block building. But from 1680 onwards his chief interests, St Paul's always excepted, lay in the disposition of large buildings composed of related blocks. Two of these, the Royal Hospital at Chelsea and the unfinished Palace at Winchester, both works for the Crown, were begun in the last few years of the reign of Charles II. Chelsea Hospital was *Ill. 129* founded by the King in 1682. The old story that he was in-

129 Chelsea Hospital

fluenced by Nell Gwyn is a myth; the moving spirit was Sir Stephen Fox, one of the Treasury Commissioners who had been Paymaster-General to the Forces and who was to be a generous benefactor to the Hospital. Charles was the first English King to maintain a regular army, though this was much disliked by Parliament, and some provision for pensioners was clearly necessary. There can be little doubt that the idea was based on Louis XIV's foundation of the Invalides in 1670; indeed, in 1677 the Duke of Monmouth asked Louis' minister, Louvois, for plans of the French hospital. Wren's plans, however, were in no sense an imitation.

130 Chelsea Hospital. Portico at end of court

The site by the river at Chelsea had been occupied by an unfinished theological college founded by James I, and the term 'college' persisted, for many references to the Hospital in the late seventeenth or eighteenth centuries speak of it as 'Chelsea Colledge'. The foundation-stone of the new building was laid by the King in February 1682, the whole building being covered by early 1685. The scheme was then enlarged to house five hundred inmates (today there are about four hundred), additional side courts being added, and the Hospital was not completed till 1691. It is the only one of Wren's major buildings for which no drawings have survived. It is therefore impossible to follow the evolution of the design, which presents several novelties. The main building consists of long and relatively narrow blocks arranged round three sides of a large court, the fourth side being open to the river. All are of equal height, and all are covered by a single sloping roof, which is not broken at the angles. The main material is brick, with stone dressings, for money was short. This is, in fact, Wren's first large-scale experiment with brick, though he had used it earlier in some of the City churches.

The key to the plan lies in the purpose of the building. The centre block contains a hall and chapel on each side of a vestibule, that is to say, features for common use, while the side blocks are the wards for the pensioners. The arrangement of these is notably humanitarian, for Wren wished the old men to have as much light and air as possible. He therefore rejected the plan of the Invalides, with its small and dark side courts. His wards, which are reached by staircases at their inner end, have a middle wall with cubicles on both sides opening on to a wide passage running the whole length of the block behind the large windows. The cubicles are partitioned in wood, and therefore give some privacy, especially as the panelling is arranged with an opening on the passage side, over which a curtain could be drawn at night. Each ward has a large fireplace in the centre of the wide, light passage, so the latter provided a place for recreation in addition to its convenience for circulation.

The logical planning of the main block, with hall and chapel, which are similar on the exterior, is not, as has sometimes been suggested, derived from a medieval college plan, though at Wren's own college, Wadham, the hall is on one side of the entrance, balanced by an antechapel (or vestibule to the chapel which then projects at a right angle) on the other. Such a plan had, however, been proposed by John Webb for an abortive rebuilding scheme for Whitehall Palace, which was certainly known to Wren. As will be seen, he was to use it again in his first project for Greenwich Hospital, and it was to be copied by other men at the Queen's College and All Souls at Oxford.

Ill. 134

Since this block is the heart of the building its importance is emphasized in the external design. The windows are large and round-headed, and in the centre, leading to the vestibule, is a portico of giant Doric columns, flanked by loggias of smaller coupled columns of the same order. The juxtaposition of the large and small orders is not entirely happy, but a precedent could be found for it in Palladio, and like so much at Chelsea, it serves a human purpose, for the loggias face south-west, and contain seats where the old men can sit in the sun. Rising above the roof behind the portico is a small tower, covered by a cupola. The tower, with columns standing out at the angles, is a variant of ideas used in the City churches, but the feature is often, and indeed rightly, criticized as being too small for the centrepiece of so large a building. Wren had wished to make it larger, and had indeed asked for permission in February 1687 to re-use one of Inigo Jones's west towers of St Paul's, which were 40 feet higher and more massive than the little cupola, but the clergy refused to allow it to be rebuilt for secular use. The mere fact that Wren could have proposed this at so late a date proves with what care the stones of Jones's work at the west end of St Paul's had been preserved in case they could be used again.

Ill. 130

Ill. 75

The long side wards at Chelsea, with their rows of square-headed windows, are broken in the centre by a curious applied portico of giant Doric pilasters. This is awkwardly handled, for

148

131 Chelsea Hospital. Council Chamber

in order to preserve the window levels the central window breaks uncomfortably into the frieze. Moreover, so important a feature suggests some change in the interior planning, such as a central staircase. But this does not occur, and the wards with their cubicles run the whole length of the block. The portico is therefore devised purely as an accent on the exterior, echoing in a flat manner the portico of the central block, and has no real connection with the plan.

Since Chelsea Hospital was Wren's first large secular building, it is not surprising that it was experimental, both in plan and elevation, and that the elevation is not entirely successful. The long ranges of plain brick are perhaps a little bleak, and the accents are not quite strong enough for the size of the court. It should perhaps be remembered that the original windows, like most windows of their time, were casements, which were changed to the present sash-windows by Robert Adam in the late eighteenth century. The mullions and transoms of the casement-windows would have been heavier than the present narrow bars, and would have altered the proportion of void to solid throughout the long fronts. The great roof, admittedly broken by dormer-windows, but still the major horizontal, giving mass and tying the whole building together, offers a

Ill. 55 strong contrast to Hooke's Bedlam Hospital or to the characteristic buildings with corner pavilions Wren had seen in France. Here, however, we can be certain that the effect was one of choice and not of chance, for in his fragmentary 'Tracts on Architecture' (which will be discussed in Chapter VIII) he makes his feelings clear: 'Fronts ought to be elevated in the middle, not the Corners; because the Middle is the Place of greatest Dignity, and first arrests the Eye; and rather projecting forward in the Middle than hollow. For these Reasons, Pavilions at the Corners are naught; because they make both Faults, a hollow and depressed Front. . . .' The date of this statement is unknown, but Wren must have formulated the idea in his mind before he built Chelsea. Most of the interiors have been little altered since Wren left them; the Chapel has fine work in wood

Ill. 131 and plaster, and the Council Chamber at the river end of the east block, formerly part of the Governor's House, has a carved overmantel by William Emmett (who worked for Wren elsewhere) which is as elaborate as any similar work by Gibbons.

The Palace at Winchester, almost contemporary with Chelsea, is perhaps the most French of all Wren's designs. During the last years of Charles II's reign, when he was striving to uphold the power of the monarchy by dispensing, so far as possible, with a contentious and often unreasonable Parliament, he was in close touch with Louis XIV, and probably planned his new Palace in the south of England, so that he would be well placed to receive French envoys. Moreover, the old Palace at Newmarket, which Charles had made much use of for sport, had recently been burnt down, and some other country-house, further from the intrigues of London than Windsor, was evidently desired by the King. John Evelyn records that the

132 Winchester Palace. Reconstruction

foundations had been begun in September 1683, and that two years later the work was 'brought almost to the covering'. But by then the King had been dead for nine months, and though part of the building was habitable, it was never really completed. It was later much altered and used for barracks, which suffered a major fire in the late nineteenth century. All that now remains are fragments from the old portico inserted in the modern building. Luckily a few original drawings and a considerable number of documents and accounts survive, also some early descriptions and an important eighteenth-century engraved reconstruction of the proposed Palace, said to have *Ill. 132* been based on one of Wren's original drawings.

Although no final plan of the whole project exists, it is certain that it was on a considerable scale. The Palace itself, set on a terrace behind a large forecourt, had, like Versailles, a gradually narrowing court leading to the centre block adorned by a giant portico and surmounted by a dome. Like Chelsea, therefore, the design emphasized the middle – 'the Place of greatest Dignity'. Like Chelsea, too, were the subsidiary accents on the side blocks, though these were more logically arranged; for where the court first began to narrow, the break was marked on each side by giant columns, with a small cupola above them. These features may perhaps have indicated the position of the two chapels which the Palace is known to have contained, but unfortunately, though a list of the rooms in Wren's writing still exists, it cannot be fitted to the existing plan, and the position of the chapels and of the great stairs cannot be determined. It is clear, however, that the resemblance to Versailles extended to the inclusion of two small courts within the main block, and a reorganization of the whole site, for a street of new houses was to run from the Palace down to the Cathedral, and a great park was to be laid out behind the Palace.

Ill. 133   The only remaining drawing by Wren for Winchester is not for the final scheme, since it does not show the giant portico. This was certainly begun, for the Grand Duke Cosimo of Tuscany presented marble pillars for it. These were given to the Duke of Bolton by George I, and removed from the site. Descriptions make it certain that the main work was of brick with stone dressings, so that the accent given by the giant columns, as at Chelsea, would have been one of colour as well as of scale. So far, however, as can be judged from the engraving, Wren still had difficulty in handling his giant order, though too much reliance should not be placed on a later reconstruction of a work which was never finished. What is interesting, apart from the extensive use of brick and stone, is the opportunity it gave for large-scale planning, an aspect of architecture which was in the future to be of great importance to Wren.

The question of large-scale planning of royal palaces inevitably leads back to Whitehall. Extension and rebuilding schemes for the King's chief palace recur almost throughout the seventeenth century, and persist in the early eighteenth century, becoming a nightmare to the architectural historian; but none

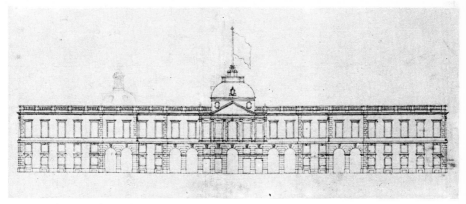

133 Winchester Palace. Elevation of court front

was ever carried out. When Charles II returned to his throne in 1660 the Palace consisted of Jones's great Banqueting House, joined to a number of rambling Tudor galleries and lodgings, running down to the river. There is evidence that on a number of occasions during his reign, Charles was hopefully considering rebuilding, though on a relatively modest scale. John Webb made many drawings for rebuilding schemes, some obviously dating from the reign of Charles I, but what appears to be his last plan, made for Charles II, was certainly known to Wren. This plan consisted of a main range, at the back of a deep court open at one end to the river. The major block was to contain the Banqueting House, a central portico next to it, and beyond the portico a replica of the Banqueting House, which was to be fitted up as a chapel. It is this which may be the source of the plan of Chelsea Hospital. Behind this main façade were two smaller enclosed courts, which would have blocked the road now known as Whitehall, and enabling the private apartments to be set at the back of the building, looking on to St James's Park. Wren produced at least one drawing for a palace roughly on this plan, for it shows the Banqueting House and its counterpart flanking a central portico. It cannot, however, be dated, though it is likely to be after his appointment to the Surveyorship in 1669.

Ill. 134

Ill. 135

153

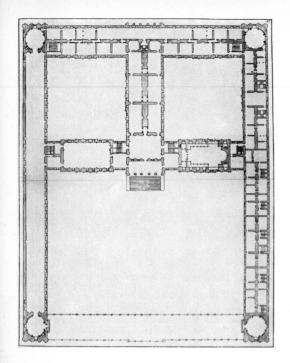

No major alterations were made to the Palace by Charles, but in the three short years of the reign of his brother, James II, considerable rebuilding took place. It was not, however, a redesigning of the whole Palace, but rather a replacement of many of the Tudor buildings with new and more up-to-date apartments. Except from the building accounts which have been preserved, and some contemporary references in the *Diary* of John Evelyn, it is difficult to get a clear picture of what was done, for the new work stood for only ten years, and then was destroyed by fire. A few of Wren's drawings for individual features remain, but the best idea of the Palace after the altera-

Ill. 136 tions can be obtained from an unfinished topographical drawing made in the early 1690s. The view is taken from the river side, with the Banqueting House in the middle distance. Then, beyond further, lower blocks, St James's Park runs back to a distant building, Buckingham House, which did not then

135 Whitehall Palace. Elevation

136 L. Knyff's drawing of Whitehall Palace

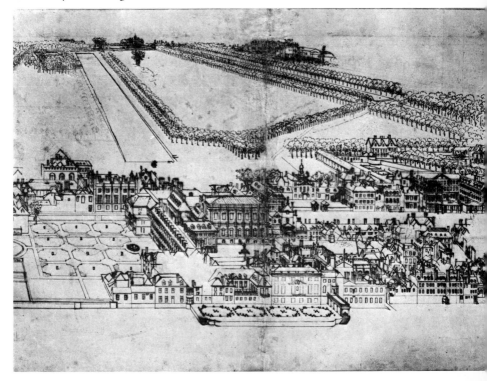

belong to the Crown. On the right, behind the avenue of trees, are the buildings of St James's Palace, while stretching back on the left is the long straight canal dug early in the reign of Charles II, to give the troops employment. The landmarks are much the same today, though Buckingham House has been rebuilt, and the Long Water became serpentine in shape when the Park was 'landscaped' by John Nash in 1828.

Wren's alterations to the Palace are mainly to the left of the Banqueting House. The long building of three storeys with dormer-windows in the roof was the new Privy Gallery. The complex of buildings behind it contained a great staircase and a new Chapel, while close to the Banqueting House the building with arcades on the lowest storey was the Council Chamber. All these buildings differed greatly from Jones's Italianate Banqueting House, built entirely of stone, for they were of brick with stone dressings. Brick had always been widely used in England, and not only for minor buildings, for Henry VIII had been content to use it when he built St James's Palace in 1532. Wren's use here is to some extent an acceptance of an English vernacular style, though with basically classical proportions; and it had great practical advantages of low cost and speed in building.

By far the most important part of the new work was the Chapel. James II was a Roman Catholic and so something very different from the plainly decorated rectangular Chapel of Chelsea was required. With much ingenuity, Wren organized a

Ill. 137
Ill. 38

difficult space by inserting columns to bring it to a long octagon, such as that of St Antholin, with a vestibule at one end and the chancel at the other. Much of the interior was painted by Antonio Verrio, an Italian who had already been employed at Windsor, the ceiling showing the Assumption of the Virgin; and a great deal of gilding was used on the decoration. In the chancel stood a great marble altarpiece, an elaborate creation with Corinthian columns in two tiers. The upper framed Verrio's painting of the Salutation, but there was also much sculpture by Gibbons and his partner, Arnold Quellin.

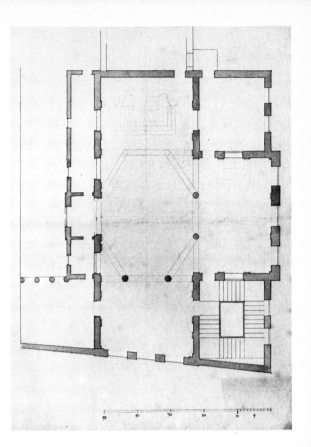

137 Whitehall Palace.
Plan of Chapel for James II

This included four standing figures, wrongly described by Evelyn as 'St John, St Peter, St Paul and the Church', two beautiful kneeling angels looking down at the altar, almost *Ill. 138* certainly the work of Quellin, and a number of reliefs of putti, probably by Gibbons. Evelyn, who was a staunch Anglican, was horrified at the Roman ceremonies, though he was honest enough to admit his admiration for the decoration of the Chapel. It was quickly dismantled after James's flight in 1688, and all that has survived of its glories is the organ now in St James's, Piccadilly, and most of the sculptured altarpiece. This was sent down to Hampton Court, and then re-erected without the standing figures in Westminster Abbey. Finally, in the nineteenth century the angels and putti were regarded as

157

unsuitable and were moved by one of the canons to the church of Burnham in Somerset, where they still remain. The standing figures, two of which are female, remained at Westminster, but since they stand unsheltered in the Canons' Garden, their surface is now so weathered that no character remains.

Ill. 136 Wren's last work at Whitehall was the fairly large building set behind a terrace on the river front. This was for the use of the Queen, and is referred to as 'Her Majesty's Privy Apartment', though on one drawing it is titled 'The Queen's New Drawing Room'. Since work was begun only in February 1688, it can scarcely have been finished by December of that year, when King James fled to France, and it was probably completed for Queen Mary II, the terrace being laid out in 1691. The garden was 'curiously adorned with greens, which cost some 1000 of pounds', and must have been a pleasant place; the covered way to the river stairs, by which the Queen would reach her barge, was also a convenience in bad weather. These stairs, curving down to the river, were the only part of Wren's Palace to survive. They were uncovered earlier in this century when the site was being excavated before the beginning of the new Air Ministry, and proved from their position how much wider the river had been before the Embankment was built.

The Queen's Apartment, for which two preliminary drawings in Wren's hand survive, continued the brick and stone style of the main new blocks for James II, and like them had sash-windows instead of casements. Sashes appear to have been first used at Windsor by Hugh May about 1680. The design is simple, but dignified, the windows being grouped in pairs, and the centre being marked by a pediment above a niche. It is, in fact, the type of building which appears frequently in the second half of the seventeenth century as a country-house, though its origins lie in the reign of Charles I. Wren was not a country-house builder, for he was too much occupied with public works, but a very small number of houses are traditionally ascribed to him. The house for Henry Guy, Gentleman of the Bedchamber of Charles II, formerly at Tring, Hertford-

138 Arnold Quellin's angel from Chapel of James II, Whitehall Palace

shire, was said in a County History published in 1700 to have
been his. It was probably as early as 1670, but in its use of
grouped windows, niches and a pediment it had something in
common with the Queen's Apartment. Winslow Hall, Buck-
inghamshire, was built in 1700 for William Lowndes, Secretary

159

to the Treasury, and Wren certainly checked the building accounts, so he may well have provided the design. This is a simpler building, without niches, though the centre again has a pediment. But such houses are very close in style and handling to many others built in England between 1660 and 1700. A number of them have from time to time been ascribed to him with no good reason except that they are agreeable. This brick and stone style, or sometimes brick alone, is often wrongly referred to as 'Queen Anne'; but it antedates the Queen's reign, which began in 1702, by some forty years, though it persisted till the Palladian revival of the 1720s encouraged even modest patrons to feel they must build in stone.

The last example of Wren's brick and stone domestic style was a town- and not a country-house. In 1708 Queen Anne granted a site adjacent to St James's Palace to the Duchess of Marlborough, who employed Wren to build her a house. Marlborough House, which was finished in 1711, was built of Dutch bricks, redder in colour than English bricks, and was relatively massive in design, with heavy coigns and a straight balustrade instead of a sloping roof with dormer-windows. Such heavy coigning is unusual in Wren's work, and suggests that he had looked with approval at its use in the Orangery at Kensington, almost certainly the work of Nicholas Hawksmoor. The house has since been considerably altered by the addition of a third storey in place of the balustrade, and a new projecting entrance on the north front.

CHAPTER SEVEN

The mature secular buildings

The accession of William III and Mary II in 1688 was to provide Wren with some of his finest opportunities, in which the experience in secular building gained in the previous ten years was to stand him in good stead.

The new sovereigns did not like Whitehall. William was asthmatic, and the damp fog rising from the river did not suit him; Mary may well have felt a little uncomfortable in her father's Palace. Some other residence in cleaner air and more pleasant surroundings was required, and very soon after the Queen's arrival in February 1689, plans were being made for two new palaces at Kensington and Hampton Court.

Kensington Palace can never have been a very satisfactory job for its architect. William had bought Nottingham House, a compact early seventeenth-century house with a good garden, and ordered Wren to enlarge it. The contract of July 1689 shows that at first four pavilions were to be built on to the corners of the old house. During 1690, however, further additions were made round a courtyard to the west of the house, *Ill. 139* and for the next few years there were constant alterations. The Queen was impatient, work was carried on too fast, and part of it collapsed and had to be rebuilt. The inside was transformed in 1691, when the King's Staircase was enlarged, and the Queen's Gallery, with its own staircase and a separate block for the maids of honour, was built. Finally, in 1695 the King's Gallery was *Ill. 140* added on the south side. It is not surprising, in view of these piecemeal additions, that the Palace had no logical plan, and the confused impression of the interior is increased by later alterations, notably the redecoration carried out for George I by William Kent. The simple exterior of brick, with its sloping roof above a strongly marked modillion cornice, is much as it

139 Kensington Palace. Clock Court

140 Kensington Palace. King's Gallery

was in Wren's time. The Queen's Gallery, with fine door-heads, large sash-windows and dormers above, would seem to be a smaller version of the Gallery built for James II at Whitehall. The exterior of the King's Gallery is rather different in feeling. It is less domestic, for there are no dormer-windows, and the heavier cornice, and above all the use of giant pilasters in brick, give it a more monumental air. It is now thought that this design may be not by Wren, but by Nicholas Hawksmoor. He had entered Wren's office in 1679 as a draughtsman, had been given increasingly responsible work, and was Clerk of the Works at Kensington from 1689 to 1696. In 1696 he was paid for making a model of the King's Gallery and also for making up the accounts. His own work throughout his career is marked by a simple grandeur, mainly obtained by mass, which fits well enough with the style of the Kensington Gallery. It is not improbable that Wren, who was extremely busy in the 1690s, might have allowed the younger man to make the design, but the responsibility for the work lay with the Surveyor; in the absence of further evidence it is impossible to judge the part played by each, and it is perhaps best to regard it as a joint design.

162

Kensington was close enough to London for the carrying on of official business, and it was to be much used as a residence by all succeeding monarchs till the 1760s. It was not enough, however, to fulfil all the wishes of William and Mary, and within two months of the Queen's arrival plans were afoot for the transformation of Hampton Court Palace. This lies on the Thames, some thirteen miles from London, and was then in open country. It was therefore less foggy than Whitehall, and gave William the opportunity of indulging his passion for hunting.

The buildings already on the site had been begun by Cardinal Wolsey in 1514, and were much extended by Henry VIII in the 1530s. The Palace had been frequently inhabited by the Tudors and earlier Stuarts. Henry VIII's gardens had been kept up and Charles II had created the canal or Long Water in the Home Park.

Wren's first designs which appear in a series of drawings, chiefly in pencil, in his own hand, are of great interest, for they show the development of his ideas beyond the earlier buildings of Chelsea and Winchester to a more Baroque style. He proposed that the whole of the old Palace should be pulled down, *Ill. 141*

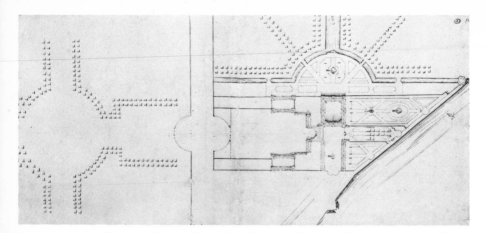

141 Hampton Court Palace. Grand layout. The River Thames is on the right, the Avenue in Bushey Park on the left, and the Long Water runs from the middle of the semicircle at the top. Henry VIII's Great Hall is opposite the end of Bushey Park Avenue

with the exception of Henry VIII's Great Hall, which was to serve as one of the focal points of the large new Palace. This would have two main axial lines, one from the north, down the great chestnut avenue to be planted in Bushey Park, and one from the west, running right through the building to the Long Water in the Home Park. Henry VIII's Great Hall stood across the end of the northern approach, and was reached through narrowing courts, thus echoing the plan of Winchester and of Versailles. It is impossible to be sure if Wren intended to reface the Hall, which is on a high basement, but the existing plan suggests that he meant to make a new entrance in the centre of the hall with, on the Park side, an elaborate flight of steps leading to it. Passages were to be left at both ends of the Hall, *Ill. 142* leading to the Great Court open at the west and so lying on the other axis. The block at the east end of this court, which the visitor would find on his left if he approached through the Hall, was the main façade of the Palace. Behind it lay a rectangular court of considerable size, very much larger than that eventually

164

built, with its east front on the gardens, the main entrance on that side being centred on the Long Water in the Home Park. In the plan of this court Wren appears to be recalling Bernini's first plan for the Great Court of the Louvre, for both plans show staircases set in rather an unusual manner, protruding from the inner angles of the court.

The elevations belonging to this first scheme are of great interest, and like the plan contain echoes of France. Moreover, on four of the drawings Wren has indicated the purpose of the rooms within and therefore a fairly complete idea of the plan of the first floor can be obtained. The drawing for the main façade on the east–west axis, called by Wren 'The Grand Front', has an impressive centrepiece with eight giant columns carrying an attic, above which is an unusual dome, with a concave drum.   *Ill. 143*

142 Hampton Court Palace. Proposed plan

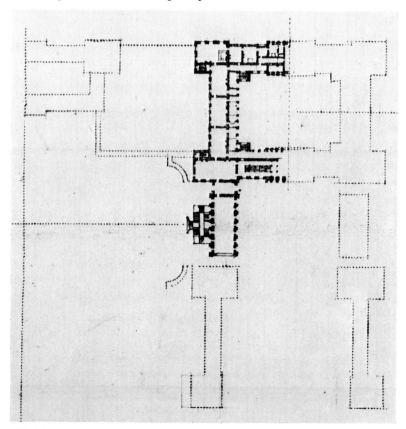

The general disposition of this central section has links with some of the designs for the east front of the Louvre, above all with François Mansart's, and it is just possible that the dome may be a rationalization of a strange feature made up of concave and convex sections which appears on the design provided for Louis XIV by Carlo Rainaldi. The centrepiece and a similar but pedimented feature on the Park front would, naturally, have been in stone, but the drawings suggest that the two-storey sections on each side were to be brick with stone dressings. Between the first-floor windows are long panels, almost certainly of stone and therefore echoing very closely, both in design and in colour, the court façade of Versailles.

The inscriptions on this drawing describe the three central openings on the ground storey as '3 Thorow visto into ye Park the midlmost looking downe ye Canall', thus stressing the basic idea of axial planning. The outer openings lead to vestibules at the bottom of the two great staircases, the King's on the right and the Queen's on the left. On the upper floor the central position was given to the Council Chamber, with its Ante-Room and Drawing-Room on either side, while drawings for the other elevations show that the King's Stair led to his apartments on the south, looking towards the river, the Queen's Apartments being mainly on the far side of the court looking over the Park.

The Palace was therefore to be on the most lavish scale, and both its carefully thought-out plan, combining it with the layout of the parks, and also the design of the elevations, show a much greater coherence than the designs for Winchester. In fact, though Wren could hardly yet know it, the inclusion of the major suite of rooms centred on the Council Chamber was unnecessary. The 'Glorious Revolution' of 1688 was followed in the next year by the passing of the Bill of Rights. This killed for ever the doctrine of the Divine Right of Kings, and henceforth power rested with Parliament. The King could no longer rule by decree, nor could he control his Ministers except by persuasion, since they were chosen from the dominant party

166

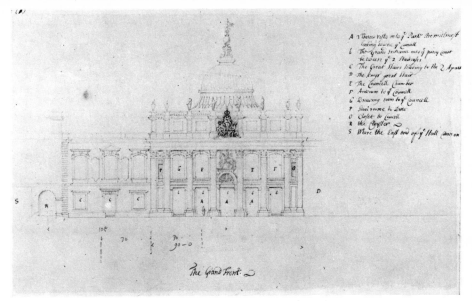

143 Hampton Court Palace. Drawing for the Grand Front

in Parliament, and were responsible to it. Government no longer followed the King from place to place, but was permanently established at Westminster. The King therefore required a palace in which he could live in such state as he desired, but it need no longer be also an office requiring space for administration.

It must quickly have become apparent that the first scheme was on too grand a scale. It would inevitably have been costly, and from its very size slow to build. It is not surprising that it was abandoned, though it is sad that this was so, for the drawings suggest that it would have been among Wren's most distinguished works. An alternative must quickly have been devised and approved, for by June 1689 work on foundations was begun. *Ill. 144* A large part of the Tudor Palace was now to be left undisturbed, *Ill. 145* though the side towards the Home Park was to be demolished, and replaced by ranges of buildings round a new court, Fountain Court, far smaller than the great court of the first scheme. The main entrance to the Palace from the west through

144 Hampton Court Palace. Air view from the south-west. The Tudor buildings remain on the left, with Henry VIII's Great Hall at the back of the second court. To the right is Wren's new building, surrounding Fountain Court

145 Hampton Court Palace. Plan of first floor

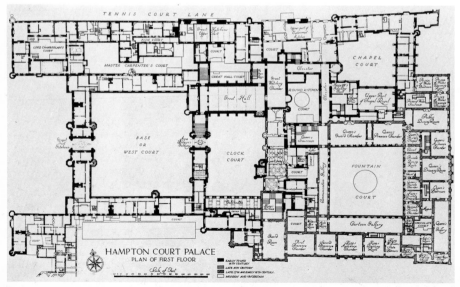

146, 147 Hampton Court Palace. Centre part of Park front and Park front from the south-east

the Tudor Gatehouse was retained, so Wren was compelled to give up all idea of axial planning. The Gatehouse and the two Tudor courts behind it are not aligned with the canal in the Home Park, so no 'visto' through the building could be arranged. Wren was therefore forced to compromise. The visitor, having crossed the two Tudor courts, the second of which has Henry VIII's Great Hall on its north side, goes through a third gateway into a relatively dark passage, which leads to the north-west corner of the cloister of Wren's new Fountain Court. After moving forward along the north side of the cloister, a right-hand turn leads to the centre of the east side, which is opposite the canal in the Park. The change of direction is skilfully handled, for the dark passage to some extent confuses the mind, and the contrasting brightness of the cloister leads the visitor firmly to the Park.

All idea of an entrance from the north was given up, indeed almost the whole of the north side of the Palace remains as in Tudor times, and there is nothing like the Grand Front of the first scheme to impress the visitor on arrival. The two great staircases originally projected on each side of the portico had now to be fitted in separately. The King's Stair rises from the south-east corner of the second Tudor court, and leads to the King's Apartments on the first floor of the south front, looking across Henry VIII's Privy Garden to the river, while the Queen's Stair is fitted into the dark passage next to the cloister.

A number of drawings for elevations exist in which the process of simplification from the first scheme to the executed *Ill. 147* building can be traced. The Park front was now the most important front. At one moment Wren hoped to have a pedimented centrepiece, with a giant order rising from ground level, and a second smaller order on the first floor articulating the whole length of the façade. Finally, the smaller order was given up, *Ill. 146* and the centrepiece reduced in scale, the columns being set on high bases, and extending therefore over the first storey only. This final alteration may have been made for reasons of cost and speed, but the availability of stone may also have been a con-

170

sideration. Wren insisted on using Portland stone, but by about 1690 the quarries were stretched in order to provide the stone for St Paul's, and he may well have realized that the less stone he required for Hampton Court the better.

The Palace as executed is therefore Wren's final work in the handling of the combination of brick and stone. It is infinitely less monotonous than Chelsea, for stone is used not only for coigns and window dressings, but also for the whole of the lowest storey, for a plain horizontal band beneath the attic windows, and for the balustrade which crowns the building. The design relies for its effect chiefly on the balance of horizontals and verticals. The basic unit of a round-headed window on the ground floor, a tall rectangular window for the main apartments on the first floor, with a circular window above it, and then the square attic window is repeated throughout the

148 Hampton Court Palace. South front

building. But this vertical pattern is controlled by the strong horizontals in the upper part of the design. Had the building been entirely of stone, more forceful lines might have been required, but the colour contrast of brick and stone strengthens the emphasis of the white horizontals. The brickwork is of exceptionally fine quality. Almost orange in colour, in contrast to the dark red Tudor brick, it is set with extremely fine joints, so that the whole surface is smooth, but with just enough variety to give it texture.

Ill. 148   The south front has slight variations in pattern, though the unit design of the Park front sets the theme. There is no major entrance in the centre, so though the idea of applied columns is retained, the centre is not further emphasized by a pediment. In the centre, at ground-floor level is a long low room used as an orangery, which requires further doors at each end. These are marked by a pleasant variation in the exterior design, for the standard unit is abandoned, the first-floor window is pedimented, and the circular windows are replaced by carved decoration.

Ill. 149   Fountain Court also repeats the standard unit, though with variations which make it a trifle fussy. All the first-floor windows have pediments, and the circular windows are set within carved decoration representing a lion's skin. This was a compliment to William III, who liked to be regarded as Hercules overthrowing the might of France. On the south side of the court the circular features are not windows, but are painted in grisaille by Louis Laguerre with the Labours of Hercules, while the pediment on the Park front echoes the
Ill. 146   theme in an elaborate group, carved by Caius Gabriel Cibber, showing Hercules triumphing over Envy. It should perhaps be noted that, though the circular unit throughout the design appears to be a window, it is on many occasions simply a blank with the window bars painted on. The reason for the false windows is that in many cases the coved ceilings of the State Apartments on the first floor reach to above the height of the windows, which if real would light only the outer surface of the cove.

This is not the only place where Wren had to use his ingenuity to get round a difficulty. The cloister of Fountain Court appears to have been begun on a design similar to that of Trinity College Library, with solid lunettes to the arches, and the floor level of the State Apartments dropped to the bottom of the lunettes. The King, however, thought the cloister too low and dark, though since he wished to preserve the height of the first-floor rooms, the floor level could not be raised to the logical position above the crown of the arch. Wren was therefore compelled to make a major alteration while the work was in progress – part of the south block being already roofed – and insert an elliptical arch under each semicircular arch, and allow this to carry the floor. It was probably while these alterations were being made that in December 1689 part of the building collapsed, two men were killed and others injured. By now a new and rather distasteful character was a prominent

149 Hampton Court Palace. Fountain Court

member of the Surveyor's Office. After the death of Hugh May in 1684, no new Comptroller had been appointed, but in May 1689 (just before Hampton Court was begun) William Talman, a country-house architect, was made Comptroller under Wren. It may well have been a political job, since Talman worked for the Whig aristocracy. He fell out with almost all his clients, and was evidently jealous of Wren. He did his best to make trouble over the accident, implying that Wren had been negligent, and on other occasions objected to the iron cramps inserted in the piers to hold them together. His antagonism must have added greatly to Wren's burdens, and it can only have been a relief to him when Talman was dismissed after the accession of Queen Anne in 1702.

Work was hurried on at Hampton Court, which may also have had something to do with the accident, but the King and Queen were impatient; though according to *Parentalia* Wren's relations with the latter were particularly happy. By February 1691 the pilasters of the centrepiece on the Park front were being erected, and by the end of that year lions' skins were being carved for the round windows in Fountain Court. Two years later the whole fabric of the King's Apartments on the south front was finished, though all the windows were not glazed, and the Queen's Apartments on the Park front were not entirely roofed. Then came a break, for in December 1694, the Queen died of smallpox, and William lost heart and stopped the work. He even commanded that a small separate building on the river, the Queen's Water Gallery, should be pulled down. Its loss is sad, for nothing similar to its interior decoration with lacquer-work and mirrors now remains at Hampton Court.

Luckily, however, the Palace did not suffer the same fate as Winchester, for after fire had destroyed Whitehall Palace in 1698, William renewed his interest in Hampton Court. Wren submitted a fresh estimate for the decoration and furnishing of the King's Apartments, consisting of the staircase, Guard Chamber, Presence Chambers, Audience Chamber, Drawing-Room, State Bedroom, Dressing-Room and Writing Closet,

150 Hampton Court Palace. Colonnade in Clock Court

while behind them, looking on to Fountain Court, was the
Cartoon Gallery, designed to house Raphael's Cartoons of the
Acts of the Apostles.

Although, as has been said, the King's Stair is situated in one
corner of the second Tudor court, Wren arranged an approach
of great dignity under a colonnade of coupled Ionic columns. *Ill. 150*
The beauty and maturity of this small work, so much more
deftly handled than the colonnade at Chelsea, is perhaps some
indication of the quality that might have been displayed in the
Grand Scheme had it been carried out. The Stair itself rises *Ill. 151*
round three sides of a rectangular hall, the walls of which were
painted by Antonio Verrio with an elaborate classical allegory
extolling the virtues of King William. It is in a fully illusionist
manner, the figures appearing in front of a painted colonnade,
which seems to enlarge the space of the hall. Similar illusionist

175

devices occur on the ceilings of many of the Apartments, where painted balustrades appear above the carved cornice, through which blue sky and floating figures may be seen.

Ill. 152 It is hard to obtain a fair idea of Wren's interiors at Hampton Court from photographs, for many of the great rooms are almost cubes, with a coved ceiling rising above. All are panelled with finely designed woodwork, and many have naturalistic carving in lighter wood by Grinling Gibbons over the chimney-pieces. Many designs by Gibbons exist, some far more elaborate than anything that was carried out. At least one must have been made for Queen Mary, for it is devised to exhibit pieces from her great collection of blue and white porcelain, much of which is still at Hampton Court. The Queen's Apartments on the Park front were largely completed for Queen Anne after William's death in 1702, when the Tudor chapel, north of

151 Hampton Court Palace.
King's Staircase

Fountain Court, was remodelled, and a fine oak reredos inserted.

Throughout Wren's building the craftsmanship of every detail is of the highest quality. The panelling is beautifully proportioned, the cornices and door-cases finely decorated, and the metal-work, both of the locks to each room and of the gates on the Park front, is superb.

It is impossible to realize the beauty of Hampton Court without some reference to the gardens, for even in the compromise plan, Palace and gardens are closely integrated. Few formal gardens of the period now remain, for most were swept away in the eighteenth-century passion for landscaping, and it is fortunate that Hampton Court did not suffer the same fate.

On the Park front Wren was able to carry out the idea which appears on the plan for the first scheme. He linked the Long

152 Hampton Court Palace. King's Bedroom. The ceiling is by Antonio Verrio, and the carving by Grinling Gibbons. The bed is contemporary

Ill. 144 Water to the Palace by placing a great semicircular parterre
between them, with a fountain in the centre. This parterre was
defined by smaller canals, and crossed by radiating paths which
become avenues beyond the semicircle. The diameter of the
semicircle was extended north and south beyond the building,
Ill. 147 the resultant Broad Walk being almost half a mile in length.
The Tudor Privy Garden was retained on the south front,
though it was terraced near the Palace. Much care was taken
over plants, two men even being sent to the Canary Islands,
though what they brought back is not recorded, and still today
the gardens in the summer are ablaze with colour. Some, but
not all, of the original garden ornaments remain. Twelve
splendid wrought-iron gates by Jean Tijou originally stood
round the semicircle, but are now at the river end of the Privy
Garden. Most of the sculpture has been replaced, but the gate-
posts at the top of the Broad Walk still have their charming
groups of boys supporting baskets made by John Nost, and
those opposite the end of the Bushey Park Avenue have two
rather dog-like lions by Gibbons.

The fire at Whitehall Palace in January 1698 saved Hampton
Court from being left an unfinished shell. For a few weeks it
must also have encouraged Wren to hope that, like the far
greater Fire of London in 1666, it would give him a major
opportunity. The whole Palace except Inigo Jones's Banqueting
House was destroyed, the latter alone being saved by most
strenuous efforts. Within three weeks Wren had surveyed the
site for rebuilding, and the diarist Narcissus Luttrell records:
'His Majestie designs to make it a noble pallace, which by com-
putation may be finished in 4 years.' It has already been seen
that Wren could, on occasion, work with remarkable speed. By
the beginning of March he produced two alternative schemes,
with their plans and elevations, though by no means all the
Ill. 153 latter are in his own hand. The smaller scheme is an elaboration
Ill. 134 of the John Webb plan discussed in Chapter VI, in which the
design of the Banqueting House is repeated on each side of a
central entrance, set at the back of an open court, with wings

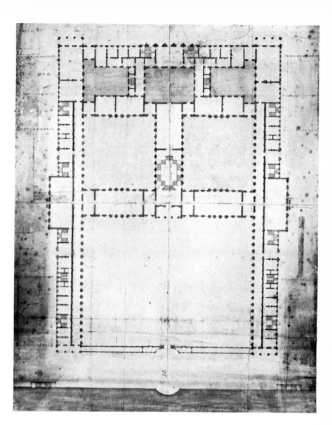

153 Whitehall Palace.
Draft plan

running down to the river. Wren's plan much enlarged the
Palace behind the Banqueting House range, so that the building
would have crossed the present street, and run back into St
James's Park. The elevations now reveal a sense of the dramatic,
which is new in Wren's architecture. The central portico has a
giant order below a heavy attic, and giant columns reappear at
both ends and in the middle of the long wings. This is yet
another example of his interest in a colossal order in the 1690s,
others being the first scheme for Hampton Court, and for a
giant portico for St Paul's, though in the Whitehall drawings
the entablatures are unusually massive, and the giant columns
are placed to gain the maximum effect. It may well be that
Wren's interest in the colossal order, which first appears at
Chelsea, was strengthened in the 1690s by the taste of his chief

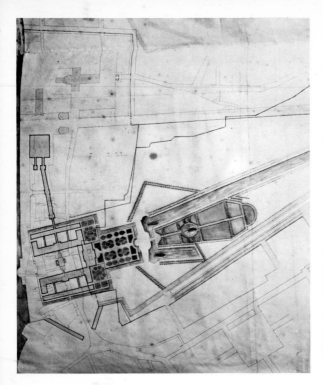

154 Whitehall Palace scheme. The palace on the left, with the Banqueting House in the centre, has flowerbeds, heavily washed in colour, between it and the Long Water. Westminster Abbey and Westminster Hall appear on the top left, with the proposed new Parliament building between them and the palace

assistant, Nicholas Hawksmoor, just beginning his independent career; but none of the Whitehall drawings are in Hawksmoor's hand.

Ill. 154   The other scheme is far more original and ambitious, for it is nothing less than an entire replanning of the whole Whitehall-Westminster area. As at Hampton Court, where the first scheme rested on the positions of Henry VIII's Great Hall and the canal in the Park, so here Wren has taken certain fixed points, the Banqueting House, the Long Water in St James's

155 Whitehall Palace. Part-elevation towards the river. The Banqueting House is shown between the two domed vesti-bules. The pedimented façades would have stood forward at the end of the wings running towards the river

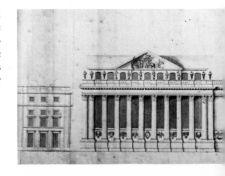

Park, Westminster Hall and Westminster Abbey as focal points in his design. The Banqueting House, now with circular vestibules at each end, was to be the heart of the Palace. But as the drawing of about 1694 shows, it was not aligned with *Ill. 136* Charles II's Long Water. To bring these two fixed features into relation with each other, Wren designed a formal garden on the Park side of the Palace, centred on the line of the Banqueting House, with beyond it a terrace from which the Long Water slanted off to the left, duplicated by a new, shorter piece of water running off on a similar angle to the right. The two were linked at the Palace end by elaborate basins containing fountains. On the Westminster side of the Palace, Wren has also introduced something new. A long gallery leads to a large rectangular building which is aligned with Westminster Hall. The building was to be a new Parliament House, and the plan reveals Wren's difficulty in tying it and its gallery to his fixed points, and his attempted solution by duplicating the entrance on the Palace side. Two small apsed buildings, the purpose of which is unknown, but which inevitably recall the churches on the Piazza del Popolo in Rome, stand at right angles to Westminster Hall, and bring this section of the layout into relation with the Abbey. Lastly, the whole area was to be treated as a precinct surrounded by a wall pierced with formal gateways, the most elaborate being that opposite the west front of the Abbey. This is indeed planning on the grand scale, and even if it is a little Utopian, it is worth studying for the skill with which Wren drew his elements together.

In the elevations which belong to this extended plan, Wren *Ill. 155* reaches the peak of his desire to create a new, more monumental style. The scale of the Banqueting House no longer plays any

part in the design, for its two clearly separated storeys have become an embarrassment. It is therefore transformed by the application of giant Corinthian porticoes, carrying straight entablatures on each of its major fronts, the circular vestibules beyond it having the same giant order, but being topped by small domes. The drawing for this centrepiece, though somewhat damaged, shows by its use of wash that Wren was deliberately using the contrast of light and shadow to enhance the dramatic effect. A giant order, running through two storeys, or sometimes a storey and a half, was lavishly used throughout the design, and parts of the building were made even richer by the application of figure or decorative sculpture.

Wren's office must have worked hard to produce drawings quickly for this exciting new project. The largest of all, more than 14 feet long, but only 18 inches high, is impossible to reproduce. It shows the complete elevation looking from the river, including the Parliament House and the long gallery, treated once more with a giant order linking it to the Palace. It appears to be drawn by William Talman, whose heavy draughtsmanship is singularly unattractive compared with that of Wren.

Wren's hopes of executing his new project must have been short-lived, for on 3 March, just six weeks after he had surveyed the site, Luttrell records that two hundred labourers were clearing the site, and that the Banqueting House was to be turned into a chapel. He continues: 'His Majesty has given directions to Sir Christopher Wren to erect a range of buildings at the end of the Banqueting House next the Privy Garden, to contain a council chamber and five lodgings for his own use; but the rest will be omitted till the Parliament provide for the same.' Inevitably, Parliament made no provision, and Wren's great project remained on paper only. It must, however, take its place in any study of his work, for it shows how his mind had moved by the late 1690s to an architecture which, both in the whole and in the parts, is at once dramatic and monumental. It is, in fact, Baroque.

156 H. Danckerts' painting of the Queen's House and King Charles's Block, Greenwich. The Queen's House is in the foreground, with King Charles's Block nearer the River Thames

The last and finest of Wren's secular buildings was the Royal Hospital at Greenwich. Again it is a story of compromise, of a first scheme abandoned; but even so it is probably the most distinguished group of buildings in England. The idea of a hospital for seamen, similar to the military hospital at Chelsea, had first been conceived by James II, who had himself seen service in the Navy, but nothing was done in his brief reign. After the victory of La Hogue in 1692, Queen Mary decided that the foundation should be made as a thank-offering and in 1694 a Royal Charter was issued.

The work of Inigo Jones in the Queen's House at Greenwich, *Ill. 156* and of John Webb in King Charles's Block, nearer the river, *Ill. 5* has been discussed in Chapter I. Wren's first plan, made in 1694, *Ill. 157* accepted King Charles's Block, and made it an integral part of the design, but ignored the Queen's House. A counterpart of

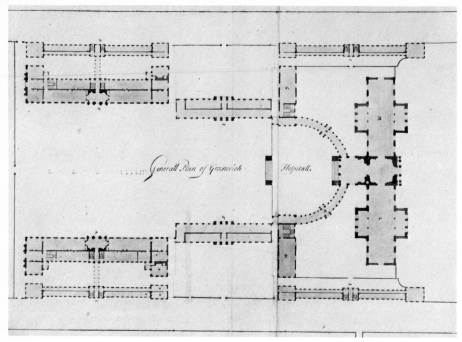

157 Greenwich Hospital. First scheme, plan

158 Greenwich Hospital. First scheme, perspective drawing

Webb's block, which was itself large-scale architecture, and therefore likely to win Wren's admiration in the 1690s, was to be built, as Webb had intended, on the east side of the larger court open to the river. Behind these two blocks the court, flanked by further buildings, narrowed slightly, and was terminated by a semicircular colonnade. In the centre of this was a great pedimented portico, serving as the entrance to a large *Ill. 158* building set at a right angle to the axis of the courts. This contained two large rooms, probably intended as the Hall and the Chapel, separated by a vestibule covered by a high dome. The view from the Queen's House would have been blocked, but Wren had achieved a long vista leading back from the river, terminating in a building grand enough to dominate the whole design. Moreover, he could have used his much-desired giant order in a splendid setting.

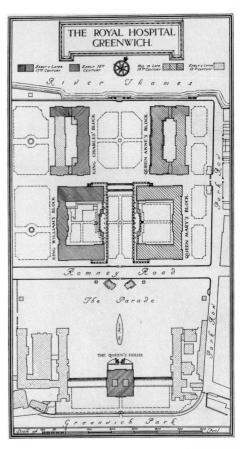

159 Greenwich Hospital. Executed plan

160 Greenwich Hospital. Air view. The Queen's House, with nineteenth-century additions, is at the top

161, 162 Greenwich Hospital. Colonnade and Chapel, and dome of the Chapel seen through the colonnade

Ill. 159
Ill. 160 The blocking of the Queen's House was not, however, acceptable, and though the Queen herself died at the end of 1694, the King rejected the plan. In January 1696, the 'Committee of the Fabrick', of which both Wren and John Evelyn were members, approved new designs to be laid before the King. In this second scheme, which was accepted, Wren was compelled to abandon all hope of a central dominating feature, for a way now had to be left through the new Hospital to the Queen's House. Though this is in itself a beautiful building, it is only two storeys high, and therefore not an adequate culmination to the view from the river. Wren, however, did his best for it, by moving his strong accents away from it, and building long and simple colonnades running up towards it. The section nearest the river was to be much the same as in the first scheme – a great open court, with King Charles's Block to the west and a replica of it to the east. Then, as in the first scheme, the court

Ill. 161
Ill. 162 narrows. But the strong accents are now placed at this point, for the Great Hall on the west and the Chapel on the east are marked by domes set on high drums. These frame the Queen's House, which stands further from the river and slightly uphill, but they do not overwhelm it. The colonnades of coupled Doric columns begin on the river side of these two buildings and, turning, run back for about 350 feet towards the Queen's House. At first Wren had intended the wards for the inmates to run off at right angles to the colonnades, three on each side, which would give the interiors the maximum of light and air; but as finally built the wards are round three sides of courts.

In the summer of 1696 work was begun, first on a narrow base block, afterwards replaced, on the outer side of King Charles's Block. In the next year these blocks were repeated on the east side of the court, and later became known as Queen Anne's Block. The Great Hall and the end of the colonnade were begun in 1698, the dome over the Hall being finished in *Ill. 163* 1704 though the interior painting by Sir James Thornhill was not completed till 1717. Before this, the idea of wards at right angles to the colonnade had been abandoned, for King William's

188

Court, behind the Hall, was begun in 1702. By now, other architects were involved. Sir John Vanbrugh replaced William Talman as Comptroller of the Works in 1702, and in 1705 Nicholas Hawksmoor, who had been Clerk of the Works since 1698, was made Assistant-Surveyor for Greenwich. A detailed discussion of their ambitious projects, or even of their actual work, is outside the scope of this book, but it seems probable that Hawksmoor, rather than Vanbrugh, was responsible for King William's Block, and that this was built during Wren's term of office. The corresponding court behind the colonnade on the east side, known as Queen Mary's Block, was not built till after 1729 mainly by Thomas Ripley, who also completed the Chapel. This last, however, was burnt in 1779, but the exterior, fortunately, preserves the original design.

In spite of the prolongation of the work, and the part played by other men, there can be no doubt that the conception is Wren's, for the setting-out of the court by the river, the placing

163 Greenwich Hospital. Painted Hall

of the Hall and Chapel with their domes, and the colonnades running back from them, are the essence of the design.

Ill. 164   Like Hampton Court, Greenwich relies for its effect chiefly on a combination of horizontals and verticals. But there the resemblance ends. Hampton Court has flat façades enlivened by a colour contrast. Greenwich viewed from the river is a stone building (though brick is used in the courts) and the façades are broken up by features giving strong contrasts of light and shade. Moreover, though horizontals and verticals predominate, there are also slanting lines of pediments echoing each other across the building, and the final accent lies in the curved domes. Here also the effect of light and shade is carefully studied. The high drums follow the pattern of the then uncompleted west towers of St Paul's, with columns, here paired, round a circular core, and groups of columns standing out above the angles of the towers below. These inevitably make a striking pattern of lights and shadows, while on the river side added complexity is given by the round window above them with its deep hood-mould

164 Greenwich Hospital from the river

cutting up into the dome. Like the twin Hospital at Chelsea,
Greenwich owes nothing to the disposition or richness of
surface ornament, but a very quick comparison shows how
Wren had grown in his mastery of architecture in the fifteen
years which divide the two. The small loggia at Chelsea may
have taught him something of the effect of plain colonnades;
at Greenwich he makes a far more imaginative use of the
motive, using its long horizontal entablature above the strong
vertical of the columns to carry the eye back to the Queen's
House, in which horizontals are the strongest accent. All Wren's
greater buildings are compromises, and though, owing to the
compromise, Greenwich may have no climax, Wren had not
lost heart, but designed a building which is not only a splendid
frame for Inigo Jones's work, but is also great architecture in
its own right. It has a clarity, a control of architectural form,
which is not found elsewhere except in the west towers and
dome of St Paul's, and which place it among the masterpieces of
English architecture.

165 David Le Marchand's portrait relief
of Sir Christopher Wren

CHAPTER EIGHT

Conclusion

The extent and variety of the executed works of Sir Christopher Wren can hardly be rivalled by those of any other architect. If to them are added the various abortive projects already discussed, the work would seem more than sufficient to fill even his long working life. They were, however, by no means the only calls on his time. For nearly fifty years he was Surveyor-General to the Crown, and in this capacity he had to deal with a stream of petitions and complaints, all of which required investigation, as well as with the supervision of a number of minor royal undertakings. Such work would nowadays be part of the activities of the Ministry of Public Building and Works; Wren had to deal with it with the help of his small staff, and it is clear from the accounts and other surviving documents that much was done by the Surveyor himself.

Many of the cases which came to him for investigation must have arisen out of differences of opinion between officials, and suggest that human nature has not changed much. In 1675 he was ordered to arrange a little room in the Green Cloth Yard at Whitehall 'for the use of the Queene's Majesty necessary woman', but since it is specified that it must be done 'so that it does not offend Mr Vice Chamberlain' it is likely that this records the end of an attempt of the Vice-Chamberlain to crush the suggestion entirely. In 1690 he was required to estimate the cost of sweeping the street outside Whitehall Palace, and at the same time to advise who should pay for it. In 1693 he dealt with a complaint about the cold in the House of Commons, which then met in part of the medieval Palace of Westminster. The windows were double-sashed on the east side, but Wren was clearly of the opinion that 'where cold was perceived it was from those who opened the windows of the passage to look out

193

on the Thames'. And in 1699 an investigation had to be made into an encroachment by the Officers of the Ordnance on the ground of the Royal Mint, then situated within the Tower of London, by which a smith, employed by both parties, was having a new house built 'in the very middle of the Mint'. These are only a few of many instances in which the Surveyor was called in to settle a dispute.

Much more work arose from petitions of individuals for permission to build, chiefly though not entirely, in the West End of London. A number of Royal Proclamations had been issued at various times in the century, some attempting to restrict the spread of the town, but others, notably those of 1667 and 1671, aiming chiefly at the regulation of the type of building. In 1671, for instance, Colonel Thomas Panton had purchased land which included two bowling greens fronting the Haymarket, and had demolished old houses. He states that his proposed new buildings would be an improvement. Wren visited the site and reported 'that the design of building shewne to me may be very useful to the Publique, especially by opening a new street from the Hay market into Leicester Fields which will ease in some measure the great passage of the Strand, and will cure the Noysomness of that part.' Panton Street still runs from the Haymarket to Leicester Square. But, though Colonel Panton was going to ease an early traffic problem, he was to be compelled to build in brick, with 'sufficient sewers and Con-veighances for the water', and the streets were to be paved. There are numerous occurrences of the same kind, but not all went through so smoothly, and an Order in Council had to be issued against inhabitants of Soho, who were without permission 'erecting small and mean habitations', which would cause 'the infecting or total Losse of the waters which by many expencefull Drains and Conduits have formerly derived from these fields to yr Majesty's Pallace of Whitehall' and would also 'choake up the Aire'. Water-supply and the interference with it was a recurring problem to the Surveyor, especially as the Piccadilly and St James's area was expanding fast.

Inevitably time had to be given to questions of minor repairs to royal buildings, large or small, out of London. Chapel Hainault Lodge in Epping Forest needed rebuilding, and the great Jacobean house at Audley End in Essex, purchased by Charles II, needed nearly £3000 to be spent on it by 1695 if it was to be saved from ruin. And there was much construction and alteration nearer home. The Royal Mews, both those on the site now occupied by the National Gallery, or those of St James's Palace, figure frequently in the books. Ice-houses in St James's Park were in 1690 so decayed that new ones must be provided; there are many papers dealing with the upkeep of the royal parks, and for the care of the rare birds already to be seen in St James's Park; and after the building of Kensington Palace the making and upkeep of the new road in Hyde Park to Kensington House fell to Wren's charge. In addition, he was responsible for stands and barriers on special occasions, such as the Coronations of James II and William and Mary, and for the funeral of Queen Mary in December 1694. Many other small tasks were part of the Surveyor's duties; those quoted are only samples of a great body of work, but they are enough to give some idea of its character.

It is also probable that on occasions Wren gave advice or even a drawing in his private capacity as an architect. His possible connection with a few domestic buildings has been discussed in Chapter VI, but he certainly made drawings for the school erected by Sir John Moore, Lord Mayor of London, at Appleby in Leicestershire, though the work was eventually carried out, with alterations, by a provincial architect. Something of the same kind may have occurred at Ingestre Church in Staffordshire built by Walter Chetwynd, a Fellow of the Royal Society. And there is a possibility that one of Wren's designs was sent to America. In 1724, the year after Wren's death, the Reverend Hugh Jones in *The Present State of Virginia*, writing of the College of William and Mary at Williamsburg, begun in 1695, stated: 'The building is beautiful and commodious, being first modelled by Sir Christopher Wren, adapted to the Nature of the Country by the Gentlemen there; and since it was burnt down, it has been rebuilt. . . .' The original College was burnt in 1705, and the only known representation of it suggests that, if Wren did indeed send a design, the adaptations of the Gentlemen in America were such that it bore little resemblance to his architecture. Although it was of brick and stone with dormer-windows in the roof, and therefore had some general affinity with English work in these materials, the proportions appear to have been clumsy, and it cannot have been exactly based on a Wren design.

Wren's long years in office, stretching from the reign of Charles II to that of George I, saw many changes, and the mere fact that he served successive monarchs without interruption proves that he was far from being a party man. On three occasions, in 1680, 1689 and 1690, he was returned as a Member of Parliament for Old Windsor, but he played no part in politics, on the last two occasions his election was challenged, and he never took his seat. His portraits, and indeed his dealings with men, which can be gleaned from the mass of the accounts of his buildings, suggest that he was essentially a temperate man. The portraits also suggest sensitivity and humour. Small in stature, slight and evidently neat in appearance, he seems to have aroused little professional antagonism except on the part of William Talman, and he was loved and admired by his friends. Evelyn invariably speaks of him as 'the incomparable Sir Christopher Wren', and Dr Robert Hooke, who was not an easy character, said of him: 'I must affirm that since the time of Archimedes there scarce ever has met in one man, in so great perfection, such a mechanical hand and so philosophical a mind.'

Ills. 1, 31, 165

The end of his long life was a sad one. His triumph had come with the finishing of St Paul's about 1710, and it has been already shown that in final small matters, such as the iron railings and the balustrade, his wishes were ignored. On the accession of George I, the office was put into commission, but Wren, who was then eighty-two, was allowed to keep the title of Surveyor-General. In 1716 he retired from the Surveyorship of Greenwich

Hospital, which passed to Sir John Vanbrugh. It seems that Vanbrugh might at that time have also become Surveyor-General, but refused 'out of tenderness to Sir Christopher Wren'. In 1718 the blow fell, and Wren was dismissed from his office. He was succeeded by a nonentity, William Benson, who quickly revealed his incompetence as an architect. In the following year Wren was called upon to answer charges of mismanagement during the years the office had been in commission. His reply is characteristic of his moderation, for he points out that he had had no power of overriding the Commissioners in their actions, but that he had 'endeavoured to doe his Majesty all the Service I was able, with the same integrity and zeal which I had ever practised.' He suggests that the Commissioners be asked to answer the charges, and ends: 'as I am dismissed, having worn out (by God's mercy) a long life in the Royal service, and having made some figure in the world, I hope it will be allow'd me to die in peace.'

This letter was written from the pleasant house at Hampton Court, overlooking the river, the lease for which had been granted to Wren by Queen Anne. He retained it to his death when it was regranted to his son, Christopher, who from 1702 to 1716 had held the office of Chief Clerk of the King's Works. Wren had a second house in St James's Street, and it was here, on 25 February 1723, he died at the age of ninety-one. The following week he was carried to St Paul's 'with Great funeral State and Solemnity', and buried in the crypt under the choir. His grave is marked by a plain black slab with the simplest of inscriptions, but later his son caused a further Latin inscription to be set up on the wall above his grave. It ends: '*Lector si monumentum requiris circumspice*' (Reader, if you seek a monument, look around you). It is the perfect epitaph.

Wren's stature as an architect is not quite easy to assess fairly. He stands head and shoulders above his English contemporaries, and so has at times been overrated. Equally, he has been underrated. The immense difficulties he faced and conquered do not necessarily make him a great architect, but they add enormously to his stature as a man. It should never be forgotten that not only was he self-trained, but that throughout his life, except for the few months in France early in his career and before he had had much experience of the problems of architecture, he never met an architect (or indeed an artist in any field) who was his equal. He therefore lacked the stimulus of rivalry, and of the discussion, which must have been general in Rome or Paris, about contemporary buildings. Moreover, since he made no other journeys, his entire knowledge of antiquity and of Italian architecture was drawn from books. Some indication of the use to which he put such knowledge has already been given; but some further attempt must be made to discover, so far as it is possible, how he thought about architecture and where his main interests lay.

There are two sources which throw some light on this, though in neither case is it complete. The first is his own collection of books and engravings, the second is the fragmentary writings he left behind him. He built up a fine library, and added to it many engravings of foreign buildings, antique sculpture, gems and coins. These, together with large numbers of his own drawings and engravings after his buildings, passed to his son Christopher. George Vertue, the eighteenth-century antiquary, notes that the younger Christopher was 'inclined once to publish much of them but some disgust happend the many plates of Architecture and buildings were already done'. After Christopher's death in 1747 the library was sold, and the rest of the collection in the next year. Catalogues of both sales exist, though the second in particular is not always very explicit.

In the book catalogue it is reasonable to suppose that all books published before Wren's death in 1723 were his. The very small number of later books included were presumably added by the son, but they are not enough to suggest that he was an eager buyer. As would be expected, Wren owned almost all the major treatises on architecture – Vitruvius (in Claude Perrault's edition), Alberti, Serlio, Vignola and Palladio. In fact he had two editions of the last, the Venetian of 1601, which he must chiefly have used in practice, and Leoni's English edition of 1715, bought near the end of his life. He also had a number of books on modern Italian architecture, and a few on French. Many more books are connected with antiquities and almost a quarter of the library was made up of books on travel, above all in Greece and the Levant. These range from Pausanias' account of ancient Greece to those of modern travellers, some of them known to Wren, such as Sir John Chardin who described his journeys to Persia and India. A number of books on English antiquities are also included, and Campbell's *Vitruvius Britannicus* of 1715, to which Sir Christopher was a subscriber. It is a good working library, but striking in the preponderance of books on every aspect of the ancient world.

The writings betray an equal interest in antiquity. They consist of five essays, all probably incomplete, which were perhaps found by the younger Christopher among his father's papers, and which were included in *Parentalia* as 'Tracts on Architecture'. They cannot be precisely dated, nor is it possible to know if all were written at the same period of Wren's life, but from a few references to his own work it seems improbable that they are very early, and indeed there are a number of hints that they must have been written by a man of experience.

The last, which seems to have been titled by Wren 'Discourse on Architecture' is a discussion, drawn from many sources, of the early history of architecture, ranging from Noah's Ark and the Tower of Babel to Solomon's Temple, the Walls of Babylon and the Tomb of Lars Porsenna, which Wren and Hooke had argued about in 1677. Naturally, it is not a consistent history, and should not be regarded as such, but Wren's practical interest in the buildings of which he had read is revealed, for instance, in his comment on the Temple of Jerusalem: 'Now it may well be inquired how in an uneven craggy country, as it is about Jerusalem, such mighty Loads of Stone could be brought. I shall give my thoughts.' And he proceeds to analyze the possible composition of the teams of workmen, and concludes that the thousands recorded as employed by Solomon were unnecessary.

Tracts III and IV also deal with antiquity. The first, obviously incomplete, discusses the use of columns, chiefly in the long porticoes in towns, while IV, which is considerably longer, discusses specific Greek and Roman buildings in some detail. Here Wren shows his ability to visualize, from engravings (probably those in Palladio), a building he had never seen, for he discusses the fall of light in the Temple of Peace (i.e. the Basilica of Maxentius), the effect on it of the omission of members of the cornice, and of the 'humble Portico and low Wings'.

Tract II starts with comments on the orders and their use, but continues with a criticism of existing architectural treatises: 'It seems very unaccountable, that the Generality of our late Architects dwell so much upon this ornamental, and so slightly pass over the geometrical, which is the most essential Part of Architecture. For instance, can an *Arch* stand without Butment sufficient.' Wren then goes on to analyze, with diagrams, systems of abutment, of vaulting and of the support of domes. Again he ranges widely for his examples, which include Santa Sophia, 'the Mosques and Cloysters of the Dervises', as well as ancient and modern buildings in Rome. It is written with the questioning mind of a scientist, not content to take on trust all that is written in books.

Tract I is by far the most interesting from the point of view of Wren's own practice. It is a series of somewhat disjointed statements on architectural design, with many warnings of errors into which an architect can fall. Whether it was conceived as an entity, and what more Wren might have added to it, is impossible to say. That it is incomplete is certain, for it breaks off in the middle of a sentence. Some at least of the statements can only be the result of long practical experience. 'The Architect ought, above all Things, to be well skilled in Perspective; for every Thing that appears well in the Orthography, may not be good in the Model, especially where there are many Angles and Projectures; and everything that is good in Model, may not be so when built; because a Model is seen from other Stations and Distances than the eye sees the Building: but this will hold universally true, that whatsoever is good in Perspective, and will hold so in all the principal views, whether direct or oblique, will be as good in great, if only this caution be observed, that Regard be had to the Distance of the Eye in the principal Stations.' There, surely, speaks the wisdom of experience, the considered view of a man who had made numberless architectural drawings, seen many of them transposed into models, either of the whole or of parts of a building, and then assessed, with a critical eye, their final creation in stone.

Many other sentences would be worth quoting in relation to Wren's architecture, but one paragraph has a special interest, for it throws a light on his relation to the thought of his time: 'Beauty is a Harmony of Objects, begetting Pleasure by the Eye. There are two Causes of Beauty, Natural and Customary. Natural is from Geometry, consisting in Uniformity (that is Equality) and Proportion. Customary Beauty is begotten by the Use of our Senses to those Objects which are usually pleasing to us for other Causes, as Familiarity or particular Inclination breeds a Love to things not in themselves lovely. Here lies the Great Occasion of Errors; here is tried the Architect's Judgment: but always the true Test is natural or geometrical Beauty.' The concept of natural or geometrical beauty, which is preferred by Wren, is classical, and is praised by many writers from Vitruvius onwards. But the idea of customary beauty appears to be unknown in classical or Renaissance theory. It was, however, very much alive in France in the late seventeenth century, where it plays its part in the conflict between the Ancients and the Moderns. Claude Perrault, in his *Ordonnance des cinq espèces de Colonnes* (1683) extols customary beauty as the measure by which modern man can profitably loosen the rigid rules of antiquity, while the argument for the Ancients was taken up by François Blondel and the Academy.

Wren certainly knew of this book late in his life, for in 1708 it was translated into English by John James as *A Treatise of the Five Orders of Columns in Architecture*. A copy of this was in Wren's library, but since James was within the circle of the Surveyor's Office, being Assistant Clerk of the Works at Greenwich from 1699 to 1718, Wren probably knew of his project from its inception. Moreover, his son and Edward Strong, the Master Mason of St Paul's, were in Paris for a time in 1698, and might have given him an account of the controversy between the Ancients and the Moderns, and perhaps even brought Perrault's book back with them. In any case the similarity strengthens the suggestion that at least some of Tract I was written late in Wren's life.

The importance of the statement is not, however, solely connected with his knowledge of French thought, but chiefly in its clear indication of his reverence for the rules of geometry and of proportion. This classical basis of all his thoughts can be seen in his finest architecture. Trinity College Library, the most beautiful of his early works, is a wonderfully successful essay on finely proportioned orders, but his personal ingenuity leads him to the device of the dropped floor without marring the clarity of the elevation. The same love of simple, classical rhythms is apparent in the drum below the dome of St Paul's, where he achieves the clean unbroken circle by putting his buttresses behind the columns at every fourth interval. His statement on perspective makes it certain that he thought in three dimensions; but it must also always be remembered that he knew modern Rome only from books, and thought in terms of clear outlines rather than in complex terms of the interpenetration of masses.

Ill. 166   The great variety of the commissions he received was both a stimulus and a danger. When in the 1680s he began to attack the problem of large-scale buildings of linked blocks he had to feel his way. It is, indeed, not until Greenwich Hospital that he shows complete control of large-scale design, and in the masterly contrast of horizontals and verticals, the placing of the pediments and the proportions of the domes he achieves a design of haunting beauty.

Finally, it must never be forgotten that he could not draw on the apparently endless financial resources of a Louis XIV or of the Roman Church. Almost all his buildings were hampered for lack of money. And it may well be that that very ability to compromise, to seek and find another solution and to get the work done, which was part of his strength as a man, was not always to the advantage of his architecture. Had he possessed the power and the arrogance of a Bernini, and the flawless taste of a François Mansart, many of his buildings would never have been accomplished. He is an uneven architect, but St Paul's and Greenwich surely entitle him to a high place even among his seventeenth-century contemporaries, and without his City churches and his brick and stone palaces England would be much the poorer.

166 C.R. Cockerell. A tribute to the memory of Sir Christopher Wren. Many of the buildings shown in this fantasy can be identified from the plates in this book. A few are included which were not carried out, or not now attributed to Wren

Chronological table

1632 Christopher Wren born at East Knoyle, Wiltshire.
·1655 Fellow of All Souls College, Oxford.
1657 Professor of Astronomy, Gresham College, London.
1661 Savilian Professor of Astronomy at Oxford; received degree of D.C.L.; Foundation Member of Royal Society.
1663 Appointed member of Commission for repair of St Paul's Cathedral.
1663–65 Pembroke College Chapel, Cambridge.
1664–69 Sheldonian Theatre, Oxford.
1665–66 Visit to Paris.
1666 Plan for rebuilding London after the Great Fire; appointed member of the Commission for the rebuilding of London.
1668 Report on Salisbury Cathedral.
1668–73 Emmanuel College Chapel, Cambridge.
1669 Made Surveyor-General of the King's Works; marriage to Faith Coghill.
1669–74 The Customs House, London.
1670–71 St Dunstan-in-the-East.
1670–73 St Vedast, Foster Lane.
1670–76 St Mary at Hill, Thames Street.
1670–79 St Edmund King and Martyr.
1670–80 St Mary-le-Bow, Cheapside.
1670–84 St Bride, Fleet Street.
1671–76 St Magnus Martyr, Lower Thames Street.
1671–76 The Monument.
1671–77 St Lawrence, Jewry.
1671–77 St Nicholas, Cole Abbey.
1672–79 St Stephen, Walbrook.
1673 The Great Model for St Paul's; Wren knighted.
1675 The Royal Observatory, Greenwich; birth of a son, Christopher.
1675–1710 St Paul's Cathedral.
1676–83 St James, Garlickhythe.
1676–84 Trinity College Library, Cambridge.
1677 Second marriage, to Jane Fitzwilliam.
1677–80 St Anne and St Agnes, Gresham Street.

1677–83 St Benet, Paul's Wharf.
1677–83 St Mildred, Bread Street.
1677–84 St Martin, Ludgate.
1677–85 St Swithin, Cannon Street.
1677–87 Christ Church, Newgate Street.
1678–82 St Antholin, Watling Street (demolished 1873).
1680–82 St Clement Danes.
1680–86 St Anne, Soho.
1681–82 Tom Tower, Christ Church, Oxford.
1681–83 Wren President of the Royal Society.
1681–86 St Mary Abchurch.
1682–84 St James's, Piccadilly.
1682–91 Chelsea Hospital.
1683–85 Winchester Palace.
1685–87 Whitehall Palace, Chapel and Privy Gallery.
1686–94 St Michael, Paternoster Royal.
1689–1702 Hampton Court Palace.
1689–1702 Kensington Palace.
1691–93 Whitehall Palace, The Queen's Apartments.
1694–97 St Vedast, Foster Lane, Steeple.
1696–1702 Greenwich Hospital.
1697–99 St Dunstan-in-the-East, Steeple.
1698 Whitehall Palace, rebuilding schemes after fire.
1698–1722 Repairs to Westminster Abbey.
1701–03 St Bride, Fleet Street, Steeple.
1704 Christ Church, Newgate Street, Steeple.
1705 St Magnus Martyr, London Bridge, Steeple.
c. 1708 St Edmund King and Martyr, Steeple.
1709–11 Marlborough House, St James's.
1713 St Michael, Paternoster Royal, Steeple completed.
1714–17 St James, Garlickhythe, Steeple.
1717 St Stephen, Walbrook, Steeple.
1718 Wren deprived of title of Surveyor-General.
1723 Died in London.
1750 Publication of *Parentalia or Memoirs of the Family of the Wrens*, compiled by Christopher Wren II.

Bibliography

This bibliography includes: I. The major architectural treatises used by Wren; II. Sixteenth- and seventeenth-century architectural books which he owned. The dates given are those which appear in the Wren Sale Catalogue of 1749, and indicate the date of the edition he owned, which may or may not have been the original publication. Such dates do not necessarily prove that he bought a book in the year of publication, though in many cases this is likely. Section III gives the most useful books on Wren.

I Architectural treatises

Vitruvius, *De architectura libri X*. The only known treatise on architecture from Roman times. MSS. were known in Italy about 1414; first printed edition probably 1486. First translation into Italian by Cesariano (Como 1521: modern facsimile announced). Finest edition by Daniele Barbaro (Venice 1556 and a Latin ed., Venice 1567) with woodcut illustrations by Palladio. Dr Robert Hooke owned a Barbaro Vitruvius in 1675, and it must have been known to Wren before he bought a French edition by Claude Perrault (Paris 1684). Modern editions by M. Morgan (Cambridge, Mass. 1914) and F. Granger (Loeb ed., London 1934).

Alberti, Leon Baptista, *De re aedificatoria*. Modelled on Vitruvius. First printed Florence 1485. Wren owned a Latin edition (Paris 1512), and his name occurs among the subscribers to Leoni's English translation which appeared only after his death (London 1726).

Serlio, Sebastiano, *Architettura*. An important treatise on antique and Renaissance designs in seven parts, published irregularly in Italy and France between 1537 and 1575. Many translations (Flemish, 1539; German, 1542; Spanish, 1552; Dutch, 1606; and English from the Dutch, 1611). Wren owned a Latin edition published in Venice in 1663.

Vignola, Giacomo Barozzi da, *Regola delli Cinque Ordini d'Architettura* (1562). Many editions and translations were made. Wren owned the French edition by C. A. Daviler (Amsterdam 1700).

Palladio, Andrea, *I Quattro Libri dell'Architettura* (Venice 1570). Many times reprinted, and owing chiefly to Inigo Jones's admiration for it, especially influential in England. Wren owned a copy of Book I only (n.d.), a Venetian edition of the whole work (1601), and the English edition of Giacomo Leoni (1715).

II Sixteenth- and seventeenth-century books

BOOKS ON ITALIAN AND ANTIQUE ARCHITECTURE

Boissardus, *De Romanae Urbis Topographiae* (1597) and *Antiquitat. Roman.* (Frankfurt 1627).

Rossi (Rubeis), *Roma vetus, Capitolii, Templorum, Amphitheatrum, Theatrorum, Circi, etc.* (n.d.) and *Insignium Romae Templorum Prospectus* (Rome 1684: the Temples are modern churches rather than ancient temples).

Rossini, *Antiquitates Romanae Notis Dempsteri* (Amsterdam 1685).

Fontana, Carlo, *Il Tempio Vaticano* (Rome 1694).

Bonanni, *Historia Templi Vaticani* (Rome 1696). These are the two most important books on St Peter's.

Desgodetz, Antoine, *Edifices antiques de Rome* (Paris 1697).

Pozzo, *Perspective* (1707: this is the English translation by John James which has an approbation signed by Wren and others).

Overbeke, *Reliquiae Antiquae Urbis Romae* (Amsterdam 1708).

FRANCE

Le Pautre, Antoine, *Œuvres d'Architecture* (Paris 1652).

Du Cerceau, *Bastiments de France*, II (1707).

Fréart de Chambray, *Parallèle de l'Architecture antique avec la moderne* (English translation by John Evelyn, 1707).

Blondel, François, *Cours d'Architecture* (Paris 1698).

Perrault, Claude, *Recueil de plusiers Machines* (Paris 1700), and *Ordonnance des cinq espèces de colonnes selon la méthode des Anciens*, Eng. trans. by John James as *A Treatise of the Five Orders of Columns in Architecture* (1708).

III Books on Wren

Wren, Christopher II, *Parentalia or Memoirs of the Family of the Wrens* (1750); section on Sir Christopher reprinted as *Life and Works of Sir Christopher Wren from the Parentalia or Memoirs by his Son, Christopher* (ed. by E.J. Enthoven, 1903). The 'Heirloom Copy', now in the Royal Institute of British Architects, has been reprinted in facsimile (1965).

The Wren Society, 20 vols. (1924–43). Indispensable for serious study. Illustrates all known drawings (except those discovered in 1951), and prints many documents and accounts. The drawings for London churches only, sold from the Bute Collection in 1951, have been published by Sir John Summerson in *Architectural History*, XIII (1970), pp. 30–42, with plates.

Webb, Geoffrey, *Wren* (Great Lives, 1937). Unillustrated, but excellent text.

Summerson, John, *Sir Christopher Wren* (Brief Lives, 1953); and *Architecture in Britain, 1530–1830* (Pelican History of Art, 4th ed., 1963), Part III, pp. 119–88.

Colvin, Howard, *Dictionary of English Architects, 1660–1840* (1954). Unillustrated, but the standard work for quick reference.

Sekler, Eduard, *Wren and his place in European Architecture* (1956).

Downes, Kerry, *Hawksmoor* (1969). For buildings such as Greenwich, where Hawksmoor worked very closely with Wren.

Illustration acknowledgments

Reproduced by gracious permission of Her Majesty the Queen: 57, 151, 152; A. C. L. Brussels: 72; Aerofilms Limited: 91, 160; By permission of the Warden and Fellows of All Souls College, Oxford: 25, 27, 83, 84, 85, 86, 92, 115, 116, 117, 120, 122, 127, 135, 137, 153, 154, 155; Copyright Architectural Press: 106; Ashmolean Museum, Oxford: 31; G. L. Barnes: 49; Courtesy B. T. Batsford, From G. H. Birch, *London Churches of the XVIIth and XVIIIth Centuries* (1896): 52; Bibliothèque Nationale, Paris: 80; British Museum: 136; Bulloz: 16; Copyright Country Life: 46; Courtauld Institute of Art, University of London: 12, 13, 55, 63, 76, 78, 82, 133, 134, 137, 142; Courtesy Faber and Faber Ltd, From Eduard Sekler, *Wren and his place in European Architecture* (1956): 32, 33, 34, 35, 36, 37, 38, 39, 40; E. J. Farmer: 51, 70, 71; Giraudon: 18, 19; Guildhall Library, London: 74; Martin Hürlimann: 96, 100, 101; A. F. Kersting: 2, 6, 14, 29, 41, 42, 45, 47, 56, 58, 60, 64, 65, 66, 68, 73, 97, 102, 119, 121, 124, 125, 130, 138, 140, 147, 149, 162, 164; Mansell-Anderson: 62; Georgina Masson: 67; Ministry of Public Building and Works, Crown Copyright: 3, 139, 144, 146, 148, 161, 163; National Maritime Museum, Greenwich: 128, 156; National Monuments Record, Crown Copyright: 79; National Portrait Gallery, London: 165; Sydney W. Newbery, Copyright Pitkin Pictorial: 43, 48, 50, 53, 99, 107, 110; Rijksdienst v. d. Monumentenzorg, The Hague: 7; Rijksmuseum, Amsterdam: 54; John Rose and John Dyble, by courtesy of the Dean and Chapter of St Paul's Cathedral: 89, 94, 95, 103, 104, 112, 114; Jean Roubier: 15; Royal Commission on Historical Monuments (England), Crown Copyright: 8, 44, 90, 113, 123, 131, 145, 150, 159; Royal Library, Copenhagen: 22; Courtesy of the Dean and Chapter of St Paul's Cathedral: 76, 77, 78, 79, 90, 91, 93, 96, 97, 98, 99, 100, 101, 102, 107, 110, 111, 113; Edwin Smith: 69, 93, 111, 126; Trustees of Sir John Soane's Museum: 55, 81, 87, 109, 141, 142, 143, 157, 158; Thomas Photos, Oxford: 1, 10; Eileen Tweedy: 5, 77, 98, 141, 143, 157, 158.

List of illustrations

English buildings, unless otherwise stated, are by Wren and in London

1 Sir Christopher Wren. Painting begun by Antonio Verrio (?1639–1707), finished by Sir Godfrey Kneller (?1649–1723) and Sir James Thornhill (1676–1734). *c.* 1706– *c.* 1724. Sheldonian Theatre, Oxford

2 Inigo Jones (1573–1652). Banqueting House, Whitehall. 1619–21. Interior

3 Inigo Jones. Banqueting House, Whitehall

4 Inigo Jones. St Paul's, Covent Garden. 1630–38. Etching by W. Hollar, *c.* 1640

5 John Webb (1611–72). King Charles's Block, Greenwich. 1664–69

6 Hugh May (1622–84). Eltham Lodge, Kent, from the north-west. 1664

7 Jacob van Campen (1595–1657) and Pieter Post (1608–69). Mauritshuis, The Hague. 1633–35

8 Sheldonian Theatre, Oxford. Plan of ground floor. 1664–69. From Royal Commission on Historical Monuments, *City of Oxford* (1949)

9 Rome. Theatre of Marcellus. Plan. From S. Serlio, *Tutte l'opere d'architettura et prospetiva* (1584 edition)

10 Sheldonian Theatre, Oxford. Interior

11 Sheldonian Theatre, Oxford. Roof truss. Engraving from C. Wren II, *Parentalia* (1750)

12 Sheldonian Theatre, Oxford, from the north. 1664–69. Engraving by D. Loggan from *Oxonia Illustrata* (1675)

13 Sheldonian Theatre, Oxford, from the south. Engraving by D. Loggan from *Oxonia Illustrata* (1675)

14 Pembroke College Chapel, Cambridge. Consecrated 1664

15 Pierre Lescot (1500/15–78). Great Court of the Louvre, Paris. Commissioned 1546

16 Versailles, *c.* 1668. Painting by Pierre Patel. Detail. Versailles Museum

17 Jacques Lemercier (*c.* 1585–1654). Church of the Sorbonne, Paris. West front and dome. 1635–42. Engraving from J.F. Blondel, *L'architecture françoise* (1752–56)

18 François Mansart (1598–1666) and Jacques Lemercier. Church of the Val-de-Grâce, Paris. West front. Begun 1645

19 François Mansart and Jacques Lemercier. Church of the Val-de-Grâce, Paris. 1645–67. Interior

20 Donato Bramante (1444–1514). Design for dome of St Peter's, Rome. Section and elevation. From S. Serlio, *Tutte l'opere d'architettura et prospetiva* (1584 edition)

21 Michelangelo (1475–1564). Design for dome of St Peter's, Rome. Engraving by E. Du Pérac, 1568–69

22 Salomon de Brosse (1571–1626). Protestant Temple, Charenton. 1623. Watercolour from F.C. Deublinger of Speyer, *Liber Amicorum* (1648). Royal Library, Copenhagen, MS Thott 434, 8°

23 Old St Paul's, London, south front. Engraving by W. Hollar, 1657. British Museum, Crace Collection

24 Jacques Lemercier. Church of the Sorbonne, Paris. Section through dome. Engraving from J.F. Blondel, *L'architecture françoise* (1752–56)

25 St Paul's Cathedral. Pre-Fire design. 1666. All Souls College, Oxford, II/7

26 'An exact Surveigh of the Streets, Lanes, and Churches contained within the ruins of the City of London, 1666'. Engraving by J. Leake, 1669, after W. Hollar, 1667. British Museum, Crace Collection

27 Wren's plan for the City of London after the Great Fire. 1666. All Souls College, Oxford, I/7

28 Claude Châtillon and Jacques Alleaume. Place de France, Paris. 1610. Engraving from C. Châtillon, *Topographie française* (1641)

29 Emmanuel College, Cambridge. Chapel range. 1668–73

30 Customs House, London. 1669–74. Engraving by J. Harris, 1714. British Museum, Crace Collection

31 Edward Pierce (c. 1635–95). Marble bust of Sir Christopher Wren. 1673. Ashmolean Museum, Oxford

32 St Bride, Fleet Street. Plan. 1670–78

33 St Mary-le-Bow. Plan. 1670–80

34 St Clement Danes. Plan. 1680–82

35 St Lawrence, Jewry. Plan. 1671–77

36 St Martin, Ludgate. Plan. 1677–84

37 St Anne and St Agnes, Gresham Street. Plan. 1677–80

38 St Antholin, Watling Street. Plan. 1678–82, demolished 1873

39 St Mary Abchurch. Plan. 1681–86

40 St Stephen, Walbrook. Plan. 1672–79

41 St Bride, Fleet Street. Interior before the Second World War

42 St Mary-le-Bow. Interior before the Second World War

43 St James, Garlickhythe. 1676–83. Interior

44 Christ Church, Newgate Street. Interior before the Second World War. 1677–87, destroyed 1940

45 St James's, Piccadilly. 1682–84. Interior

46 St Clement Danes. Interior since rebuilding

47 St Lawrence, Jewry. East façade

48 St Lawrence, Jewry. Interior since rebuilding

49 St Benet, Paul's Wharf. 1677–83

50 St Mary Abchurch. Interior since restoration

51 St Mildred, Bread Street. Interior before the Second World War. 1677–83, destroyed 1941

52 St Anne and St Agnes, Gresham Street. Interior before the Second World War and subsequent alteration

53 St Martin, Ludgate. Interior

54 Jacob van Campen. Nieuwe Kerk, Haarlem. Interior from east to west. 1645–49. Drawing by P.J. Saenredam, 1650. State Print Room, Rijksmuseum, Amsterdam

55 Robert Hooke (1635–1703). Bedlam Hospital, Moorfields. 1675–76, demolished c. 1816. Engraving. Sir John Soane's Museum, London

56 St Stephen, Walbrook. Interior

57 Canaletto (1697–1768). London and the Thames from Somerset House Terrace looking towards the City, c. 1746–50. Royal Collection. Reproduced by gracious permission of Her Majesty the Queen

58 St Mary-le-Bow. Steeple. 1670–80

59 St Mary-le-Bow. Steeple and section. From Wren Society, vol. IX, plate XXXV

60 St Mary-le-Bow. Doorway at base of tower. 1672

61 François Mansart. Hôtel de Conti, Paris. Doorway. c. 1645. Engraving from J.F. Blondel, L'architecture françoise (1752–56)

62 Antonio da Sangallo the Younger (1485–1546). Model for St Peter's, Rome. c. 1540–46. Museo Petriano, Rome

63 John Webb (1611–72). Design for an ideal church. Worcester College, Oxford, I/47a

64 St Bride, Fleet Street. Steeple. 1701–03

65 Christ Church, Newgate Street. Steeple. Completed 1704

66 St Vedast, Foster Lane. Steeple. 1694–97

67 Francesco Borromini (1599–1667). S. Ivo della Sapienza, Rome. View from courtyard. 1642–50

68 St Michael, Paternoster Royal. Steeple. Completed 1713

69 St James, Garlickhythe. Steeple. 1714–17

70 St Stephen, Walbrook. Steeple. Completed 1717

71 St Magnus Martyr, London Bridge. Tower. Completed 1705

72 Pieter Huyssens (?) (1577–1637). St Charles Borromeo, Antwerp. Tower. c. 1620

73 St Martin, Ludgate. Steeple. 1677–84

74 Ruins of Old St Paul's. View towards south-west, showing south transept and nave. Drawing by T. Wyck, c. 1672. Guildhall Library, London

75 Ruins of Old St Paul's. West front. Drawing by T. Wyck. Bodleian Library, Oxford, Gough Maps, vol. 20, f. 2 v

76 St Paul's Cathedral. First Model, north side. 1670. St Paul's Cathedral Library

77 St Paul's Cathedral. First Model, looking east. St Paul's Cathedral Library

78 St Paul's Cathedral. Great Model, from the north-west. 1673. St Paul's Cathedral Library

79 St Paul's Cathedral. Great Model, interior looking east. St Paul's Cathedral Library

80 François Mansart. Design for a Bourbon chapel, Saint-Denis. 1665. Bibliothèque Nationale, Paris

81 St Paul's Cathedral. Great Model, plan. 1673. Engraved by B. Cole. Sir John Soane's Museum, London

82 John Webb. Design for a Greek cross church. Worcester College, Oxford, I/40

83 St Paul's Cathedral. Warrant design, plan. Accepted 1675. All Souls College, Oxford, II/10

84 St Paul's Cathedral. Warrant design, south side. All Souls College, Oxford, II/13

85 St Paul's Cathedral. Warrant design, west end. All Souls College, Oxford, II/11

86 St Paul's Cathedral. Warrant design, sectional drawing. All Souls College. Oxford, II/14

87 St Paul's Cathedral. Plan of cathedral as executed. Engraving by T. Bowles. Sir John Soane's Museum, London

88 St Paul's Cathedral. Cross-section through choir. Measured drawing by Arthur F.E. Poley. From Arthur F.E. Poley, St Paul's Cathedral (1927)

89 St Paul's Cathedral from the south-east

90 St Paul's Cathedral. Back of screen wall, showing buttresses above aisle roof (before cleaning)

91 St Paul's Cathedral. Air view from the south-west

92 St Paul's Cathedral. Design for south side. All Souls College, Oxford, II/29

93 St Paul's Cathedral. West front, sculpture above window at base of north tower. c. 1695

94 St Paul's Cathedral. Sculpture below window on south transept to east of portico, by Grinling Gibbons. 1694

95 St Paul's Cathedral. South transept pediment with the phoenix carved by Caius Gabriel Cibber. 1698–99

96 St Paul's Cathedral. South transept front

97 St Paul's Cathedral. West front

98 St Paul's Cathedral. Drawing for giant order at west end. c. 1690–94. St Paul's Cathedral Library, I/50

99 St Paul's Cathedral. Circular stair in south-west tower. c. 1705

100 St Paul's Cathedral. Upper part of Dean's door carved by William Kempster. 1705

101 St Paul's Cathedral. South-west tower. 1705–08

102 St Paul's Cathedral from the south

103 St Paul's Cathedral. Detail of drum of dome

104 St Paul's Cathedral. Detail of niche in drum of dome

105 St Paul's Cathedral. Cross-section looking east. Measured drawing by Arthur F.E. Poley. From Arthur F.E. Poley, St Paul's Cathedral (1927)

106 St Paul's Cathedral. Isometric section of dome. Detail from drawing by R.B. Brook-Greaves in collaboration with W. Godfrey Allen

107 St Paul's Cathedral. Interior looking east

108 St Paul's Cathedral. Central space looking north-west. From T. Malton, Picturesque Tour (1792)

109 St Paul's Cathedral. Central space looking north-east as originally planned. Ink drawing by A. and A.W. Pugin (?). 1828. Sir John Soane's Museum, London

110 St Paul's Cathedral. Choir-stalls by Grinling Gibbons. 1696–98

111 St Paul's Cathedral. South choir aisle, screen at rear of choir-stalls

112 St Paul's Cathedral. Bishop's throne by Grinling Gibbons. 1697

113 St Paul's Cathedral. Chapel of St Michael and St George with screen by Jonathan Maine

114 St Paul's Cathedral. Wrought-iron gates on north side of choir, by Jean Tijou, 1698, with modern baldacchino behind them

115 Senate House, Cambridge. Elevation. 1674. All Souls College, Oxford, I/55

116 Trinity College Library, Cambridge. First scheme, plan. All Souls College, Oxford, I/41

117 Trinity College Library, Cambridge. First scheme, elevation. All Souls College, Oxford, I/42

118 Andrea Palladio (1508–80). Villa Rotonda, Vicenza. Elevation and section. Engraving from A. Palladio, *I Quattro Libri dell'Architettura* (1570)

119 Trinity College Library, Cambridge, Nevile's Court. Begun 1676

120 Trinity College Library, Cambridge. Design for longitudinal section and elevation towards river. All Souls College, Oxford, I/45

121 Trinity College Library, Cambridge, river front

122 Trinity College Library, Cambridge. Pen and ink sketch for library bookcase and desk. All Souls College, Oxford, I/48

123 Trinity College Library, Cambridge. Alcove showing desk

124 Trinity College Library, Cambridge. Interior

125 Tom Tower, Christ Church, Oxford. Upper part by Wren. Begun 1681

126 The Monument, London. Completed 1676

127 Mausoleum for Charles I. Elevation. 1678. All Souls College, Oxford, II/92

128 Royal Observatory, Greenwich. 1675. Etching by F. Place, *c.* 1676

129 Chelsea Hospital. 1682–91. Engraving by B. Cole from W. Maitland, *History of London* (1756)

130 Chelsea Hospital. Portico at end of court

131 Chelsea Hospital. Council Chamber, carved by William Emmett

132 Winchester Palace. 1683–85. Engraved reconstruction from J. Milner, *History of Winchester* (1798)

133 Winchester Palace. Elevation of court front. 1683? City Museums, Winchester

134 John Webb. Whitehall Palace, plan. *c.* 1664? Devonshire Collection, Chatsworth, Chatsworth 57. Reproduced by permission of the Trustees of the Chatsworth Settlement

135 Whitehall Palace. Elevation. After 1669? All Souls College, Oxford, II/106

136 Whitehall Palace. Drawing by L. Knyff (?) *c.* 1694. British Museum, Department of Prints and Drawings

137 Whitehall Palace. Plan of Chapel for James II. ?1685–86. All Souls College, Oxford, II/Special No 7

138 Arnold Quellin (1653–86). Angel from Chapel of James II, Whitehall Palace. 1686. Burnham-on-Sea Church, Somerset

139 Kensington Palace. Clock Court. *c.* 1690

140 Kensington Palace. King's Gallery, perhaps in collaboration with Nicholas Hawksmoor. 1695

141 Hampton Court Palace. Grand layout. 1689. Sir John Soane's Museum, London

142 Hampton Court Palace. Proposed plan. 1689. Sir John Soane's Museum, London

143 Hampton Court Palace. Drawing for the Grand Front. 1689. Sir John Soane's Museum, London

144 Hampton Court Palace. Air view from the south-west

145 Hampton Court Palace. Plan of first floor. From Royal Commission on Historical Monuments, *Middlesex* (1937)

146 Hampton Court Palace. Centre part of Park front. 1689–1702

147 Hampton Court Palace. Park front from the south-east. 1689–1702

148 Hampton Court Palace. South front. 1689–1702

149 Hampton Court Palace. Fountain Court. 1689–1702

150 Hampton Court Palace. Colonnade in Clock Court

151 Hampton Court Palace. King's Stair painted by Antonio Verrio (?1639–1707). *c.* 1700

152 Hampton Court Palace. King's Bedroom. *c.* 1700

153 Whitehall Palace. Draft plan. 1698. All Souls College, Oxford, V/10

154 Whitehall Palace. Scheme for Whitehall. 1698. All Souls College, Oxford, V/2

155 Whitehall Palace. Part elevation towards the river. 1698. All Souls College, Oxford, V/4

156 Queen's House and King Charles's Block, Greenwich. Painting attributed to H. Danckerts, c. 1670. National Maritime Museum, Greenwich

157 Greenwich Hospital. First scheme, plan. 1694. Sir John Soane's Museum, London

158 Greenwich Hospital. First scheme, perspective drawing. 1694. Sir John Soane's Museum, London

159 Greenwich Hospital. Executed plan. 1696. From Royal Commission on Historical Monuments, *East London* (1930)

160 Greenwich Hospital. Air view

161 Greenwich Hospital. Colonnade and Chapel. 1696–1702

162 Greenwich Hospital. Dome of the Chapel seen through the colonnade

163 Greenwich Hospital. Painted Hall. 1702–17

164 Greenwich Hospital. View from the river

165 David Le Marchand (1674–?1726). Ivory portrait relief of Sir Christopher Wren. c. 1723. National Portrait Gallery, London

166 C. R. Cockerell (1788–1863). A tribute to the memory of Sir Christopher Wren. Watercolour, 1838. Collection Mrs B. J. Crichton

Index

Numbers in *italics* are those of illustrations. The Chronological table, Bibliography and List of illustrations have not been indexed.

ALBERTI, Leon Battista, 72, 198
Amsterdam, OosterKerk, 63–4
  Synagogue, 64
Anne, Queen, 160, 174, 176, 197
Antwerp, St Charles Borromeo (Jesuit Church), 77, *72*
Appleby (Leics.), Sir John Moore's School, 195
Audley End (Essex), 195

BARBARO, Daniele, 15, 52
Barrow, Dr Isaac, 133, 135, 137
Bathurst, Dr Ralph, 24–5
Benson, William, 197
Bernini, Gianlorenzo, 25–6, 126, 165, 203
Bird, Francis, 113
Bletchingdon (Oxon.), 8, 44
Blondel, François, 201
Borromini, Francesco, 74, 112, 115, 118, *67*
Bramante, Donato, 31–2, 36, 72, 89, 93, 102, 113, 119, 143, *20*
Browne, Edward, 25
Browne, Sir Thomas, 25
Busby, Dr Richard, 8

CAMBRIDGE, 133, 140
  Emmanuel College Chapel, 40–1, 71, 145, *29*; Pembroke College Chapel, 23, 40, *14*; Peterhouse Chapel, 40; Senate House, 133, *115*; Trinity College, 133–40, 142, 173, 202, *116–17, 119–24*
Campbell, Colen, 199
Campen, Jacob van, 63, *7, 54*
Canaletto, 67, *57*
Cartwright, Thomas, 70, 80

Catherine of Braganza, Queen, 10
Cerebri Anatome (Willis), 10
Chantilly, 25
Chapel Hainault Lodge (Epping Forest), 195
Charenton, Temple, 32, 53, *22*
Charles I, King, 7, 14, 84, 142, 144, 153, 158; Mausoleum 142–4, *127*
Charles II, King, 8–10, 16, 37, 42, 44, 82, 85–7, 92, 96, 132, 142, 144–7, 150–4, 156, 158, 163, 181, 195–6
Chetwynd, Walter, 195
Chiese di Roma (Falda), 74, *111*
Cibber, Caius Gabriel, 110, 172, *95*
Clare (Cleere), Richard, 88
Cleere, William, 83, 87
Coal tax, 40, 45, 105
Coghill, Faith, 44
Colbert, 26
Coleshill (Berks.), 16

De Architectura Libri X (Vitruvius), 15, 49, 52–3, 198
Denham, Sir John, 16, 33, 42
De re aedificatoria (Alberti), 72
Descartes, 9
Diary (Evelyn), 36, 46, 48, 154
Diary (Hooke), 45, 49, 64
Diary (Pepys), 48
Doogood, Henry, 80

EAST KNOYLE (Wilts.), 7
Elements of Architecture (Wotton), 16
Elizabeth I, Queen, 11, 16
Eltham Lodge, (Kent), 18, *6*
Ely Cathedral, 8, 36

Emmett, William, 80, 150, *131*
Evelyn, John, 8, 19, 32, 36–7, 46, 48, 90, 132, 150, 154, 157, 188, 196

FALDA, 74, 111
Fano, basilica, 53
Fell, Bishop, 145
Fitzwilliam, Jane, 44
Flamsteed, John, 144
Fox, Sir Stephen, 146
France, 16, 25, 31–2, 36, 42, 72, 90, 102, 109, 150, 165, 198, 201
Fréart de Chambray, 132
Fulkes, Samuel, 80, 105–6, 114

GEORGE I, King, 152, 161, 196
Gibbons, Grinling, 59, 90, 109–10, 114, 126–7, 129, 140, 150, 156–7, 176, 178, *94*, *110*, *112*
Great Fire, 37, 71, 81, 83, 120, 142, 178
Gresham, Sir Thomas, 9
Grove, John, 80
Grumbold, Robert, 140
Guarini, Guarino, 31
Guy, Henry, 158

HAARLEM, Nieuwe Kerk, 63, *54*
Hague, Mauritshuis, 18, *7*
Nieuwe Kerk, 64
Hampton Court Palace, 157, 161, 163–80, 190, *141–52*
Hawksmoor, Nicholas, 106, 112, 160, 162, 180, 189, *140*
Henri IV, King, 39
Henry VIII, King, 156, 163–4, 170, 180
Holder, William, 7–8
Holland, 49, 61, 63–4, 78, 80, 90
Hooke, Dr Robert, 38, 45, 49, 52, 60, 63–4, 84, 90–1, 111, 140, 142, 150, 196, 199, 55

INGESTRE Church (Staffs.), 195
Istanbul, Santa Sophia, 200
Italy, 11, 13, 15–16, 85

JAMES I, King, 147
James II, King, 105, 154, 156–8, 162, 183, 195
James, John, 130, 202
Jerusalem, Temple of, 199
Jones, Rev Hugh, 195
Jones, Inigo, 11–17, 28, 33, 47, 59, 72, 81, 84, 89, 93, 96–7, 102, 107, 112, 143, 148, 153, 156, 178, 183, 191, *2–4*

KEMPSTER, Christopher, 80, 105–6
Kempster, William, 114, *100*
Kent, William, 161

LAGUERRE, Louis, 172
Latham, Jasper, 103

Laud, Archbishop, 84
Lemercier, Jacques, 28, 36, *17–19*, *24*
Leoni, Giacomo, 199
Le Pautre, Antoine, 90
Le Raincy, 25
Lescot, Pierre, *15*
Le Vau, Louis, 26, 137
Liancourt, 25
London
  Bedlam Hospital, Moorfields, 63, 140, 150, 55; Buckingham House, 154, 156; Chelsea Hospital, 145–53, 156, 163, 171, 175, 179, 183, 191, *129–31*; Christ's Hospital, 55
  Churches: Christ Church, Newgate Street, 55, 74, *44*, *65*; St Anne's, Soho, 45; St Anne and St Agnes, 61–2, 64, *37*, *52*; St Antholin, Watling Street, 61, 156, *38*; St Benet Fink, 61; St Benet, Paul's Wharf, 59, 78, *49*; St Bride, Fleet Street, 52–3, 55, 57, 73, 93, *32*, *41*, *64*; St Clement Danes, 45, 49, 57, 59, *34*, *46*; St Edmund King and Martyr, 64; St James, Garlickhythe, 54–5, 75, *43*, *69*; St James's, Piccadilly, 45, 57, 84, 157, *45*; St Lawrence, Jewry, 58–9, *35*, *47–8*; St Magnus Martyr, 77, *71*; St Margaret, Lothbury, 78; St Martin, Ludgate, 61–2, 78, *36*, *53*, *73*; St Mary Abchurch, 60, *39*, *50*; St Mary at Hill, 61–2, 64; St Mary-le-Bow, 53, 67, 70–3, 78, *33*, *42*, *58–60*; St Michael, Paternoster Royal, 75, *68*; St Mildred, Bread Street, 60, *51*; St Nicholas, Cole Abbey, 78
  St Paul's Cathedral, 16, 32–8, 42, 45–6, 64, 67, 75, 78, 80–133, 145, 171, 179, 190–1, 196–7, 202–3, *57*, *87–114*; Chapels, 105, 110–11, 114, 129; Commission 1663–66 (Pre-Fire Commission), 33, 36, 85, *25*; Commission for rebuilding, 86–7; Convocation House, 83, 85, 87–8; Dean and Chapter, 81, 83; Dean's door, 114, *100*; dome, 113, 118–22, 132, 191, *89*, *91*, *102–6*; First Model, 84–8, 96, 139, *76–7*; fittings, 126–7, *110–14*; Great Model, 87–93, 96, 105, 124, *78–9*, *81*; interior, 122–30, *107–114*; Model Room, 84, 88; Old St Paul's, 14, 19, 32, 81–4, 87, 120, 148, *23*, *74–5*; Royal Warrant 1668, 82; Royal Warrant 1675, 92, 96, 102, 104, 107; Warrant design, 93–7, 102, 107, 110, 122, 124–5, *83–6*; west front, 112–13, *97*; west towers, 75, 106, 113–16, 118–20, 190–1, *101*
  St Paul's, Covent Garden, 14–15, 28, 47, *4*; St Peter, Cornhill, 64; St Stephen, Walbrook, 64–7, 75, 80, 104, 125, *40*, *56*, *70*; St Swithin, Cannon Street, 61; St Vedast, Foster Lane, 74, 118, *66*
  City, 37–9, 45, 47–8, 67, 83, 103, *26–7*, *57*; Commission for rebuilding the City (1667),

214

40, 81; Rebuilding Acts, 37, 40, 45
City Churches (*see also* Churches), 45–81,
96, 103–5, 133, 147–8, 203; Commission
for rebuilding the City churches, 45, 103;
Commissioners for new churches 1708, 48
Customs House, 42–3, *30*
Greenwich: Hospital, 148, 183–91, 196,
202–3, *157–64*; King Charles's Block, 17,
23, 183–6, 188, *5*, *156*; Observatory, 144–5,
128; Palace, 16, 17, 23; Queen's House, 14,
16, 183, 185, 188, 191, *156*, *160*, *164*
Gresham College, 8–9, 38; Haymarket,
194; Kensington House, 195; Kensington
Palace, 160–3, 195, *139–40*; Monument,
142, *126*; Nottingham House, 161; Panton
Street, 194; Royal College of Physicians,
63–4
St James's Palace, 37, 156, 160, 195; Queen's
Chapel, 14, 28
St James's Park, 153–6, 179–81, 195; Ice-
houses, 195; Long Water, 156, 180
St James's Street, Wren's house, 197
Westminster Abbey, 37, 45, 157–8, 181;
Westminster Hall, 181; Westminster, Palace
of, 37, 193; Westminster School, 8
Whitehall, New Scotland Yard, 44; Palace,
11–14, 37, 43, 59, 84, 148, 152–9, 161, 163,
174, 178–81, 193–4, *134–8*, *153–5*; Ban-
queting House, 11–13, 17, 59, 102, 107,
143, 153–4, 156, 178–82, *2–3*; Chapel for
James II, 156–9, *137–8*; Council Chamber,
156; Gallery for James II, 162; Long Water,
181; Parliament House, 181–2; Privy
Gallery, 156; Queen's Apartment, 158–9;
rebuilding schemes 1698, 178–82, *153–5*
L'Orme, Philibert de, 15
Louis XIII, King, 27
Louis XIV, King, 146, 150, 166, 202
Lowndes, William, 159
Luttrell, Narcissus, 178, 182

MAINE, Jonathan, 80, 110, 129, *113*
Maisons, Château of, 27
Mansart, François, 25, 28–9, 31, 70, 89–90,
166, 203, *18–19*, *61*, *80*
Marlborough, Duchess of, 160
Marshall, Joshua, 96–7, 102–4, 106
Mary II, Queen, 112, 158, 161–3, 166, 174,
176, 183, 188, 195
May, Hugh, 16, 18, 42–3, 158, 174, *6*
Michelangelo, 31, 36, 89, 93, 102, 114, 119,
144, *21*
Moore, Sir John, 195

NASH, John, 156
Newton, Sir Isaac, 10, 144
Nost, John, 178

Oeuvres d'Architecture (Le Pautre), 90
Office of Works, 16, 42–3, 193
Oliver, John, 103–4
Ordonnance des cinq espèces de Colonnes (Per-
rault), 201
Oxford, 8, 10, 19, 24, 40–1, 81, 96, 133; All
Souls College, 8, 36, 89, 92, 135, 148;
Christ Church, Tom Tower, 141, 145, *125*;
Queen's College, 148; St Mary's Church,
19; Sheldonian Theatre, 19–22, 40, 71, 133,
8, *10–13*; Trinity College, 24–5; Wadham
College, 8, 148

PALLADIO, Andrea, 11, 14, 133–6, 148, 198–
200, *118*
Panton, Colonel Thomas, 194
Parallels (Fréart), 132
Parentalia (Wren), 10, 22, 25, 46, 55, 85–6,
91–2, 106, 112, 174, 199
Paris, 25–32, 34, 39, 48, 90, 109, 198; Collège
de France, 26, 137; Hôtel de Conti, 70, *61*;
Hôtel de Sully, 109; Invalides, 146–7;
Louvre, 26, 109, 165–6, *15*; Place de France,
39, *28*; Saint Paul-Saint Louis, 109; Sainte
Anne-la-Royale, 31; Sainte Marie-de-la-
Visitation, 31; Sorbonne church, 28, 36, *17*,
24; Val-de-Grâce, 28–9, 124, *18–19*
Peake, Robert, 15
Pepys, Samuel, 48
Perrault, Claude, 49, 52–3, 198, 201–2
Phillips, Andrew, 52
Pierce, Edward, 44, 72, 80, 103–4, *31*
Pietro da Cortona, 111
Porta, Giacomo della, 31
Portland stone, 102, 106, 112, 124, 171
Pratt, Sir Roger, 16, 33, 85–6
Present State of Virginia, (Rev Hugh Jones), 195
Principia (Newton), 10

Quattro Libri dell'Architettura (Palladio), 11,
134
Quellin, Arnold, 156–7, *138*

RAINALDI, Carlo, 166
Ripley, Thomas, 189
Rome, 39, 198, 200, 202
Colosseum, 22; Marcellus, Theatre of, 19,
22, 139, *9*; Maxentius, Basilica of (Peace,
Temple of), 55, 200; Pantheon, 107; Peace,
Temple of (*see* Maxentius, Basilica of);
Piazza del Popolo, 39, 181; S. Agnese in
Piazza Navona, 118; S. Ivo della Sapienza,
67; Santa Maria della Pace, 111; St Peter's,
30–2, 36, 72, 88–9, 93, 126, 144, *20–1*, *62*;
S. Pietro in Montorio, Tempietto, 102,
113, 143
Royal Society, 9–10, 19, 24–5, 40, 195

215

Rubens, Sir Peter Paul, 13
Ryswick, Peace of, 106

SAINT-DENIS, Bourbon Chapel, 90, *80*
Salisbury Cathedral, 41, 46, 66, 141
Sancroft, William, 81–2, 87, 96
Sangallo, Antonio II da, 72, 89, *62*
Scamozzi, Vincenzo, 134
Serlio, Sebastiano, 15, 19, 23–4, 31, 107, 133, 198, *9, 20*
Shaw, Sir John, 18
Sheldon, Gilbert, 19
Sixtus V, Pope, 39
Smith, Bernard, 105
Storey (Story), Abraham, 64
Streeter, Robert, 22, 88
Strong, Edward, 80, 104, 106, 129, 202
Strong, Thomas, 96–7, 102, 104, 106

TALMAN, William, 174, 182, 189, 196
Tangier, 10, 19
Thornhill, Sir James, 130, 188–9, *1, 163*
Tijou, Jean, 105, 122, 130, 178, *114*
Tillison, John, 87
Tompson, Colin, 70
Tracts on Architecture (Wren), 150, 199–202
Treatise of the Five Orders of Columns in Architecture (James), 202
Tring Manor (Herts.), 158

VANBRUGH, Sir John, 189, 197
Vaux-le-Vicomte, Château of, 27
Verneuil, 25
Verrio, Antonio, 156, 175, *1, 151*
Versailles, 27, 151–2, 164, 166, *16*
Vicenza, Villa Rotonda, 134–5, *118*
Vignola, Giacomo da, 15, 198

Vingboons, Philip, 60
Vitruvius, 15, 49, 52–3, 198, 201
Vitruvius Britannicus (Campbell), 199

WALLIS, Dr John, 22
Ward, Dr Seth, 9, 41
Webb, John, 14, 16–17, 23, 28, 33, 42, 72, 148, 153, 178, 183, 185, *5, 63, 82, 134*
William III, King, 112, 161, 163, 166–7, 172–8, 182, 188, 195
Williamsburg, William and Mary College, 195–6
Willis, Dr, 10
Winchester Palace, 145, 150–2, 163–4, 166, 174, *132–3*
Windsor, Castle, 43, 150, 156, 158
    Mausoleum for Charles I, 142–4, *127*
Winslow Hall (Bucks.), 159
Wise, Thomas, 103, 129
Wolsey, Cardinal, 141, 163
Woodroffe, Edward, 45, 87, 89, 103
Wotton, Sir Henry, 16
Wren, Sir Christopher, and the Royal Society, 9–10; as scientist, 8–10; character, 145, 196; journey to France, 25–32; knighthood, 44; library, 198–9; report of May 1666, 33–4; Savilian Professor of Astronomy, Oxford, 9, 40; writings on architecture, 26–7, 57, 66, 199–202; *1, 31, 165*
Wren, Rev Christopher, 7
Wren, Christopher (son), 10, 44, 46, 86, 106, 197–9, 202
Wren, Jane, 44
Wren, Matthew, 7–8, 10, 24, 36, 40
Wren, Stephen, 10
Wren, William, 44
Wren Society, 43